Amazon FBA

Achieve Your Financial Freedom: A Complete Guide to Build a Successful Passive Income Online Business with Amazon FBA (Private Label vs Retail Arbitrage)

Gabriele Undig

Table of Contents

Table of Contents

Introduction

Chapter 1: General Overview of Amazon FBA

How Amazon FBA Works

The Process of Acquiring a Product from Amazon FBA

Order Fulfillment

Safety of Buying on Amazon FBA

Pros and Cons

The Difference Between Amazon FBA and Amazon

Features of Amazon FBA

Chapter 2: Why People Prefer Amazon FBA as the Basic Profitable Online Business

The Comfortable and Smooth Running of the System

Amazon Provides Supports Especially Customer Service to All of its Members

Amazon FBA Provides a Powerful Logistics Within Its Website

Amazon Has Got an Accessible Mode of Payment

Amazon Has Unlimited Preferences in Terms of Payments

Provisions of Excellent Products with High Quality

Chapter 3: How Does Amazon FBA Create Financial Freedom

- Amazon FBA Allows You to Sell Your Product Using Its Trademark
- You Can Create Private Label All of Your Products Within the Amazon

Retail Arbitrage

- You Can Work as Their Delivery Associate
- You Can Be an Amazon Affiliate
- You Can Sell Handmade to Amazon

Merits and Demerits of Amazon FBA

The Merits of Amazon FBA

- Payment Preferences Are unlimited
- High Product Quality
- Powerful Logistics Within the Website
- Delivery Time Is Apparent
- Availability of Shipping Discounts
- Management of Returns
- Customer Service Management
- Excellent Unlimited Storage Space

Demerits of Amazon (FBA)

- Fulfillment by Amazon Costs Money.

Long-Term Storage Fees.

You May See More Returns.

Product Prep Can Be Stressful.

Complicated Tracking Process of the Inventory

Chapter 4: Details on How to Choose Profitable Product (Private Label)

The Rank of Sales

Profit for Each Sale

Product Size

Gated Brands

Brands That Are High Risk

Value of the Product

The Return Rate of the Product

Product Price History

Amazon Categories

How to Harmonize Product with Brand

Chapter 5: Define the Product for Sale in Retail Arbitrage

Products Allowed in Amazon

Avoid Selling Counterfeit Products.

Try as Hard as Possible to Sell New Products

Avoid Big Brands Such as Nike, Apple and Much More

You Must Use Your Trademark on Different Goods You Are Retailing

You Can Only Sell Post Priced Items

Don't Sell Used Conditioned Products

    Defective or Damaged Units

    Registered Products with the AMAZON

All Products Being Sold Must Comply with the Policies.

Don't Sell Duplicated or Reproduced Items.

You Can Only Sell Suitable Products

Chapter 6: Techniques to Help You Make a Powerful and Perfect Launch of a Product

Evaluation of Market and Product

Customer Involvement

Ideas Validation

Build Your Audience and Community

Use Amazon Formula for Writing a Mock Press Release

Improve Your Organic Visibility

Various Promotions Leading to Sales

    Flash Sales

    Buy A Product Get One Free

    Coupons and Discount with Purchase

    Recurring Sales

Tripwire

Chapter 7: Reasons Why People Prefer Amazon Retail Arbitrage Instead of Private Label Method

The Merits of Retail Arbitrage Which Makes It Preferable

Capital

Profit-Making Period

Reduced Volatility

Retail Arbitrage on Amazon

Reasons Why People Prefer Amazon Retail Arbitrage

Private Labeling

Disadvantages of Private Labeling

Low Orders

Dead Stock

Perception from Consumers

Private Labeling Trading on Amazon

Disadvantages of Selling Private Labels on Amazon

Chapter 8: Understanding of Retail Arbitrage on Amazon

How Retail Arbitrage on Amazon works

Reasons Why Customers Pay More on Discounted Prices

Your Items Are Easier to Purchase

You Deliver Your Products Quickly and on Time

- Your Products Help in Polishing the Customer's Reputation
- Your Products Have Lower Costs of Ownership
- You Have Friendly Customer Service
- Having a Likeable Personality to the Customers
- Customers Need Something Besides Your Products from You
- The Customer Is Experiencing Rapid Expansion

Tips on How You Can Implement Discounts Profitably
- Defining Your Objectives
- Segmenting Shoppers and Tailoring Offers Accordingly
- Ensuring That Your Timing Is Right

How Can You Use Discount Pricing Strategies to Increase Sales?

How Can You Make Customers to Pay Full Prices on Discounted Prices?

Goals You Should Aim at Achieving When You Offer Discount Pricing to Your Customers
- Acquiring New Clients
- Increasing Your Sales
- Gaining Repeat Clients
- Doing Away with Old Inventory

Various Strategies and Business Models Used in Amazon

Amazon Business Strategy

   Amazon FBA

   Amazon Affiliate

   Reselling

   Dropshipping

   Manufacturing

   Private Label

   Retail Arbitrage

   Liquidation

Amazon strategy

   Amazon Customers

   The Focus on Technology

   Competition Factor

   Media Sales

   Marketing

Chapter 9: Tips and Tricks to Earn Passive Income with Retail Arbitrage

Types of Passive Activities:

Significance of Passive Income

Tips on How to Earn Passive Income with Retail Arbitrage

Prefer Scanning for Several Items While Sourcing

Try Asking Several Questions About the Products You Are Sourcing

No More Comfort Zone

Never Overlook the Oversize Items

You Should Be Nice

Concentrate on the Overlooked Items

Change Your Sourcing Time

Don't Overlook Common Items

Prefer Specific Focus

Be Keen on Your Specialties

Conclusion

Introduction

The world population is growing at an alarming rate leading to an enormous demand for goods and services. The supply of products and, however, is moving at a slow pace. Many people are resorting to online buying and selling to quench their thirst for different products. More, there are needs we have to meet whether the goods and services are scarce. Necessities like food, water, shelter, and even clothing consider them as basic needs. Unfortunately, at some point, we can meet their demands due to low supply from the main contributors. As a result, many are looking for other alternatives such as online buying and selling.

Surprisingly, online buying and selling is becoming very popular, and creating a platform where people can easily acquire goods and services. Fortunately, these platforms are very many. The best ones are listed below:

- Amazon - this is where millions of people across the world view your products. Both customers and sellers throng this site for various reasons but mainly relating to selling and buying goods.
- eBid - this site consists of low fees

- cQout - this one of the best sites, especially within the United Kingdom. That is, it comprises of almost 57 countries.
- eBay - this has over 150 million users in the whole world.
- Folksy - it is a rapidly growing site for market purposes
- Etsy - a unique site for selling, and buyers always feel happier about the site.
- Rakuten - this is a Japanese site for eCommerce purposes.
- Gumtree - this one deals with ads, and most of the occasions, it attracts over 8 million people per month.
- Preloved - this site involves items for kids. It is where you can get everything concerning young children.
- iStock - the best site where you can sell our photographs.

All in all, people are now turning into major online sites for their daily acquisitions of goods and services. Many students and teachers are finding it accessible even to purchase books online and wait for their shipment within a specified period. That is, the purchase becomes much more comfortable without any form of pressure from the salespersons.

Therefore doing your selling and buying from an online platform has several benefits that will help even forget about ordinary buying and selling. That is where both sellers and consumers do meet. Some of these benefits we can list them below for easy understanding. Online buying and selling have the following advantages, which include:

- Cost savings in cases of fuel and saving on time
- Availability of various varieties of goods and services
- We do not have pressure to buy these products physically
- You can also make a quick comparison of the products being offered
- Convenience in terms of purchasing

However, online trading is not always a bed of roses. Both consumers and sellers under a server issue concerning this trade. On most occasions, they will experience vendor fraud where the seller becomes a fraudulent here. That is, he may receive the cash and fails to deliver the item you have just purchased. Therefore, these and other various problems have become a significant challenge within online trade, thus prompting people to go slow on this particular form of business. Fortunately, not everything is gone. Other sites are working daily to redeem the lost faith of the customers and the seller.

A good example is Amazon FBA. The Fulfillment by Amazon has come up with various solutions to solve all the online buying and selling problems. Amazon is struggling as hard as possible to redeem back the lost hope of the online trade, and because of this, many people are shifting from other sources to Amazon. The following are major reasons as to why people are now turning into Amazon:

- **Product Quality:** The product quality has been an issue since time memorial. Many sellers are using pleasing and attractive pictures to attract customers who will end up buying goods and services. However, at the consumer level, the quality standard being presented to them was not the one within the display. Amazon has come up with guidelines on how to control the quality of its products. One way is the introduction of the FBA, which literally means Fulfillment by Amazon. In this case, you will realize all goods and services being offered have to undergo through this model of fulfillment. The site will only display those items that have passed here. Meaning, they will be of a high standard.

- **Powerful Logistics:** The logistics used here by several online traders are just a big mess. That is cases of poor delivery, barring of websites, and much more is becoming a major challenge in the online trade. Sometimes, the deliveries end up missing, and that means a consumer can wait for quite some time to get the ordered item. However, at that time may be the use of that product is no more. Sometimes, the packaging becomes so poor that the quality of the product reduces along the supply chain. That is, here comes a case where the seller gave out high-quality products, and these products get destroyed by those handling. The Amazon FBA has the right way of keeping all the tabs of logistics, and this will allow it to keep all records and delivering and acquiring all the ordered items on time. That is, Amazon FBA has inventory management solutions that control the stock, their deliveries, and much more. Cases of returns are never an issue with the outlaid quality checks up through the FBA.

- **Delivery Time is very clear:** Amazon has a clear channel of delivering its message to its customers. As a result of this, many people are turning to it as among the best online trading site. In Amazon, immediately your product is packed, you will receive a message indicating all the required information.

- **Payment Preferences Are unlimited:** Most sites have listed the debit cards they always allow. In most cases, buyers or sellers will find it hard when their preferred mode of payment is not listed. However, this problem is no longer an issue with the Amazon FBA. That is, Amazon has an e-security system such as TRUSTe, which allows the website to have the full trust of the consumers. This will results in large sales since consumers can order various products without limitations.

The Amazon FBA has various benefits that we cannot list all of them here. However, you need to understand that this online trading site is better as compared to other websites. In this platform, you can also make more sales in terms of advertising and even buying merchandise and reselling them in retail form. In the end, you will be able to realize much profit in the case of a vendor. Consumers, too, are highly benefiting since they can purchase high-quality goods.

Therefore, it is now well clear that Amazon FBA has the power to help you achieve your goals in online trading. That is whether you go there as a buyer or as a vendor. And because you realize over 150 million people have already shifted to Amazon and enjoying its benefits. Most of these people are making positive reviews of Amazon on different sites. Therefore, you, too, can make it. Amazon is very convenient, and its accuracy in terms of handling the products has increased a notch higher, making it a leading online site for business.

Fortunately, with the quality of rich information being offered by Amazon, I would highly recommend you for this book. As I have done my part, I would like to assure you that when you fully implement all the information in the various chapters, you will automatically stick to Amazon as your best and favorite online trading site. That is, with Amazon, you will never hear issues of missing invoices, hidden costs, unclear website policies, complicated navigation, annoying interfaces, and overlapping of goods and services. Also, the delay in delivering a specific product or picking a fault product for returns will be much easier.

Chapter 1: General Overview of Amazon FBA

Amazon FBA is one of the best online trade platforms we have so far in our life. In a layman's language, we would say that it's an e-commerce platform that is operated and owned by Amazon. Amazon enables third-party vendors or sellers to make sales or opt for using goods on a fixed price and do it on the online marketplace. However, this is only done in conjunction with the offerings within the Amazon.

In a quick view of this online segment, you realize the third patty sellers embrace this advantage and give it a shot. That is, they gain access to the customers within the Amazon. Remember, as mentioned earlier, Amazon attracts over 150 million people in the last financial years. As a result of this, the workload of having more inventories will never be an issue since the sellers can supply their goods and services to this platform. However, you need to note that all these products being offered here have to undergo a strict quality checkup to satisfy the quality standard expected by the consumers.

All the items within this online trade platform undergo some fulfillment. That is, no single product can be delivered on this platform without a quality checkup. Quality involves checking on the brands, packaging, and much more. This is made possible by the two segments within the Amazon, which include fulfillment by the merchant (FBA), or sometimes by the Amazon itself through fulfillment by the Amazon (FBA). However, in this chapter, we aim to know much about fulfillment by Amazon, which has caused lots of shifts in the field of online trade. Therefore, in FBA, vendors can store their products in FBA centers, and all other services will be handled by Amazon, such as customer services and even shipping.

In this situation of handling the goods and services, you realize Amazon will have to charge the third-party merchants. That is a referral fee, which is comprised of a slight percentage equated from the sales price. At the same time, sellers or vendors will have to part with some fees, especially for picking, packing, and even those charges related to weights of the products. In most cases, the third-party accounts for almost over 30% of the total annual sales made by Amazon in the financial year of 2016. However, this figure has been rising due to more inductions of new sellers within the platform. That is, many sellers were able to create more Amazon accounts, which enabled them to increase their sales within the platform.

Amazon has got strict rules and regulations. The rules act as strict policies that govern and regulate its operations. Within the rules, you can enter Amazon in three ways. That is, you can get yourself and start selling in this platform using retail arbitrage, private label, or even in a situation where you are dealing with the wholesale products. Therefore, Amazon FBA is in a position of handling all your products whether you are there through retail arbitrage or, as a private label, and you will be accorded all the benefits Amazon usually gives its members. Some of these benefits start from picking, packing, and even shipping your orders from where you are to the relevant customers. Again, in Amazon, you are free to register your item with your brand name, or you use the brand name of Amazon. In this situation, it allows you to have that flexibility of your goods and services. Remember, there are several reasons behind going for the Amazon brand name or deciding on using your brand name. That is, in some situations, you will realize that several sellers are offering the same products, and if all of you decide to use the same brand name, then you might end up not realizing the massive volume of sales.

However, this only happens when you have a few followers who are yet to know much about your existence in the market. Though, in a situation where your brand is known all over the world, then you can create some distinction of your products within the Amazon FBA so that your followers will not waste a lot of time going through the huge volume of the advertised products.

As a result of that, you will be in a position to realize huge gains with your name brand. That is, the level of saving time with the Amazon platform is awesome. In most cases, this will take only two days in shipping. Meaning, many sellers will have their products listed on the platform as early as two days. The shipping of the product to the consumer will also take less time as far as the goods have been ordered. In the end, it works best for both the involved parties.

Fortunately, to increase sales in Amazon, the platform will have to use their prime logo. Here, customers will have a good understanding of whoever is handling the products. That is, in case of anything, then the online company will be held accountable for the risk incurred since it is the one handling the packing, any form of delivery, and even the customer service sectors. More so, Amazon will also handle the returns of the products in case of poor quality, which was not expected by the customer. By doing all these, you will realize that an increase in your productivity since you are left with extra time to concentrate on other issues. Hence, it will lead to the growth of your business. All these will create or establish some level of financial freedom within you.

Also, Amazon has a way of saving some costs. That is, there are no hidden costs in Amazon since shipping fees and packing fees are well stated in one invoice. Nonetheless, this one reason behind huge followers in terms of customer base Amazon is having. However, it is good to note that Amazon is one of the most searched and advanced fulfillment platforms all over the world due to its ability to pick, pack, provide customer services, and also to ship the products to relevant customers.

How Amazon FBA Works

Amazon FBA is a surprising story, especially when you look at the beginning. It offers everyone an astonishing success journey, which instills in us the morale of even working hard. Amazon began by selling only books, but later on, its expansion led to the diversification of other products. Today, you will find everything that you want on Amazon. Amazon is providing a platform where sellers and buyers can interact and exchange goods and services. With the help of retail arbitrage, a consumer can order items in low quantity.

Therefore, the influx of people in Amazon is due to the following reasons:

- Competitive prices in Amazon, especially when all products of the same genre are displayed together for selling.
- Excellent customer service since Amazon boasts of 24/7 online customer care that are ready to handle all your queries concerning every product.
- Amazon has improved its shipping process, where it is now as fast as possible. It is now making sure that the consumers or buyers can wait for lesser days for their deliveries.
- There is the presence of effective marketing, which is digitally managed. This has allowed easy and quick operations of the online trading company.
- The wide selection of Amazon products is giving Amazon's buyers and consumers a more comprehensive view of all the goods and services being offered. In this sector, you will realize the customers have a choice to make in terms of selection.

The Process of Acquiring a Product from Amazon FBA

The initial stage of acquiring a product here is to visit the **Amazon** website. In case you don't have an account, you can create one since it's free. Your account is then personalized to give it a unique experience different from others.

The moment you have spotted a product you would wish to buy, you can click Add to your Shopping Cart. From that point, you have to check out. This will take you to a new page where your details are filled for easy shipping. That is, these details include billing and shipping information. Once you are free with all these, you are required to choose your desired shipping alternative. Once you are through, hit the final confirmation button. All these will complete your order.

Order Fulfillment

Once you submit an order, Amazon starts working. Always, orders from third party vendors are sorted out to Amazon, leading to a cut of those sales. However, the larger percentage gets themselves in the warehouses of the Amazon. Remember, it is good to note that these warehouses are spread all over the world. Amazon uses specific algorithms that play a major role in their predictions. That is, this algorithm can predict the number of orders and even their types.

It is good to note that fulfillment centers and algorithms are some of the most differentiators between online retailers and Amazon. Their primary function is to increase the speed of deliveries and also supply cheaper products to customers. These are attributes that other online retailers are not having.

After identification of the product, it will be picked and packed then taken to the waiting truck for deliveries. The whole process will only take a few minutes, and the moment the customer resends back the notification, the product will be loaded on the delivery truck.

Safety of Buying on Amazon FBA

Other online sectors are having issues with the breaching of security. However, in the Amazon FBA, things are different. The online trading business understands that the only way to have full trust from the buyers is one of the best techniques it is using to have more success in the future. That is, its future success lies with the buyers, and because of this, they have to provide a platform where buyers will never have a doubt. As a result, you can always upload payment information on this site, and just by one click, you will be able to begin buying the products. Sometimes, you can also use this to have recurring orders without payment complications.

Some years back, many people had many concerns when it comes to Amazon. That is its way of handling cookies within its website. In this case, Amazon is very aggressive in terms of cookies usage. We need to understand Amazon prefers cookies when it's tracking its customers, especially on other websites. It will use this information to deliver ads, send emails, to customize the offerings. However, when it comes to payment, Amazon uses SSL or Secure Sockets Layer. This system offers maximum protection of any payment, which arises from third party sources.

Again, many people have that feeling of the touching product before making any payment. However, with Amazon, someone should not worry about the quality off the merchandise. Remember, in case the product ordered is substandard, then you have a right to return it since it has a free return policy. This is not only to its prime members but also to every user with an account with Amazon. In this case, if the buyers have an issue with the product delivered to them, a full refund process will be initiated without any question. This strategy has made many people have the complete trust of the Amazon FBA.

Pros and Cons

Amazon FBA is the leading online site for trading. Both sellers and buyers are thronging in this site to either acquire products or to sell their products. Amazon has a necessary foundation that can help you realize your financial freedom if you implement it very well. Remember, it is not only the sellers who can benefit much but also the buyers who are continually getting into the sites to acquire goods.

This online trading platform has many benefits that are already mentioned in various chapters. Some of them include the following:

- Best return policy which is free
- Perfect and excellent customer service
- Good security of both the consumers and vendors
- Perfect logistics
- Low prices of products which allow customers to purchase goods with ease
- Amazon FBA has customized the experience in the field of online trading.
- Amazon offers products in large quantities, which gives a clear comparison of the prices. This will lead to a cost saving of the products.

- It has the right way of reducing procurement complexity.
- Always strives towards customer's empowerment by providing essential information concerning a particular product. This includes delivery options of the products, price transparency, ratings of all sellers, which allow you to look at the best-rated sellers, and more so, it gives a clear picture of the product ratings.
- Amazon creates a foundation where sellers can interact and sell their products while on the other hand, creating access to all buyers, both prime Amazon members, and new members.

However, a coin has two sides, which speak a lot about all types of business, whether it is online or the normal one where buyers and sellers meet to exchange their goods and services. That is not always a perfect business will lack reasons as to why some hate it. Many people have a lot of grievances when it comes to the mode of operations of Amazon. That is, it has a ruthless way of dominating all online retails. Since it has a larger market share and low prices of its products, Amazon tends to mistreat its workers by underpaying them. More so, Amazon has the audacity of squeezing sellers. That is, it makes sure that all sellers are placed in a specific niche of its website. Meaning, at the end of the day, some sellers might fail to make sales due to overcrowding of similar goods.

Furthermore, smaller retailers who cannot manage competition are being squeezed out of the website. This leads to loss of employment and income to workers who are not skilled. Again, most retailers are very young. By eliminating them or squeezing them out, they will become jobless again. This will not only reduce their per capita income but also reduces the general per capita of their corresponding countries. Again, without enough income of these youths, they might end up doing evil related activities such as doing drugs.

The Difference Between Amazon FBA and Amazon

Amazon FBA has the ability to provide buyers with the needed access, especially to multiple products. Remember, due to competitions, some sellers put restrictions and other regulatory policies, which will prevent the buyers from accessing, thus making comparisons.

It again provides vital information concerning how you can manage a one-stop shopping, especially across its vast products. Therefore, this will save both time and resources, such as money and much more.

Amazon FBA can offer techniques for controlling your expenses within the site. This allows a smooth run of your purchase and at the same time, gives a clear direction of what goods to spend on and which ones are profitable. As a result of the mentioned above, Amazon has got some requirements in its features category that you must comply with to make the best sales and acquiring of the products.

Features of Amazon FBA

- It has a free two-day shipping process
- It has the ability to purchase different orders and customize them accordingly. Again, it will be able to give out analytics reports.
- Approval flow of works and provisions of multi-user accounts
- Discount oriented on eligible products
- Excellent pricing model
- Qualified organizations are tax exempted

Amazon FBA is becoming popular in most countries, with

youths venturing and investing in this platform. Its ability to transfer money into your account has enabled it to be labeled as the best online trading site. Amazon will transfer money into your account twice per month.

Therefore, anyone can eventually start an Amazon FBA, which can be done within less than a month. In this scenario, you have to come up with your brand and try as much as possible to have much freelancing to do the foundation work. Starting the Amazon FBA business is not costly at all, but again you should know it is not easy to start. For you to survive, you require patience, aggressiveness, capital, and various inventories.

Chapter 2: Why People Prefer Amazon FBA as the Basic Profitable Online Business

The population is growing at an alarming rate, with the demands of goods and services becoming very high. The supplies of these products are low, leading to the creation of online sectors to cater to all these. Many people are now ending up sorting themselves through the online trade since this will deliver the ordered item at your doorstep. More so, many sellers have found a platform where they can sell their products without any headaches. In the end, these vendors will realize enough financial freedom as they sell and stock most often.

However, not all websites or online trading eCommerce are eligible to satisfy your needs. Some online traders are part and parcel of frauds and malicious thefts who will end up stealing from the customers. Others will charge hefty fees on their respective shipping and, more so, handling of their inventories. Sadly, this will also lead to poor quality of products since they might have poor handling of products.

Unfortunately, this will lead to poor quality at the buyer level. In this case, consumers will end up consuming poor-quality products, which might threaten their lives. Even if they apply for return policies, it might take quite number days, or sometimes this might fail to occur. The consumer will end up incurring losses, and this will lead to negative reviews on the goods and services being offered on that online trading business. All in all, sellers will also have to undergo some huge substantial losses. Since most buyers will shift their preferences from that online trade due to their poor-quality service. At the end of everything, it will be a lose/lose situation of the seller, online company, and the buyer.

However, not all are gone. Online trading is one of the best sites where you can make excess profits if you are very keen. We have several sites such as Amazon, eBay, Etsy, and much more. In all the categories, Amazon has been tested and proved to be the most profitable online trading business. Eventually, you need to know that being the most profitable online company is not easy. That is, it comes with pain and suffering. You will need to persevere and compete vehemently with other huge competitors. An online website for trading purposes will have to work extra hard to redeem the faith and trust of its followers.

There are several ways that Amazon outdoes its competitors, especially in the online sectors. One of them is the availability of advertising TV channels of Amazon. Through this, Amazon will have to advertise its products, which will end up reaching substantial traffic within a second. All these will translate to a massive amount of sales, which will reflect on the maximum profit gained by the sellers.

Amazon has other reasons, which make it a darling online site for trading. Below are some solid reasons as to why people will always prefer Amazon for their online trading escapades:

The Comfortable and Smooth Running of the System

Getting into Amazon and starting to earn with it is very simple. The only way to go is to start by creating an FBA account, which will enable you to have all your inventories fulfilled. A fulfilled stock is one that will have logos, trademarks of the Amazon, and other required policies. The over 150 million people will always see this that the Amazon is commanding.

You can then go ahead by making additions to the Amazon catalog for selling. You can do this one by one or in bulk, depending on your ability to acquire products. After this, you can click on the eCommerce ready, which will allow your products to be delivered to consumers after an order is made. You can then carry out shipping to the warehouse of Amazon. However, this can be done by Amazon itself, which will later charge a small fee. At some points, you can involve discounted large carriers where you will get some discounts along the process. Discounts will enable you to save some cash that you could have used in transportation. This will increase your financial gains since it has reduced the total cost price of the whole process.

After all these, the ordering process will occur, and Amazon will do everything to make sure your products are dispatched to specific customers. The money will be credited to your Amazon account. This will also give you a convenient time of doing other tasks such as making changes to the reviews, especially the ones that had burning issues about the products. The free shipping also will help you save more money hence leading to excess profits. This is one of the reasons as to why many people prefer Amazon as compared to other online trading business. This ability to meet some of your expenses always acts as an incentive towards its members.

Amazon Provides Supports Especially Customer Service to All of its Members

Most online trading business will never offer a 24/7 customer care service as Amazon. As a result, this will be handled by the seller, who will incur some charges such as traffic charges, plus much more. However, Amazon will handle all these on behalf of its customers. These roles include initiating quick refunds and returns, and more so, handling customer inquiries. Fortunately, both sellers and consumers will remain with enough time to concentrate on profitable errands, which will help them to achieve much.

Amazon FBA Provides a Powerful Logistics Within Its Website

Logistics has been an issue ever since the exchange of goods and services started. In traditional trades such as barter trade, you will realize that those who had excellent and perfect logistics outdid the rests. That is, they ended up making more profits while others experienced huge losses. Our grandfathers who managed to be in that trade could keep good records like what to exchange, what to keep, and how to get the next stock. All this information was crucial since they managed them to deliver to their inappropriate manner. However, in modern days, the logistics used here by several online business people are just messy, unlike what Amazon FBA is offering. That is cases of barring of websites, poor delivery, and much more is becoming a major or a difficult challenge in the online business.

In most cases, the deliveries and other paper works end up missing, and this implies that a consumer has to wait for quite some time to get the requested products. Unfortunately, at that time may be the use of that product is no more. Sometimes, the packaging becomes so poor that the quality of the product reduces along the supply chain. That is, here comes a case where the seller gave out high-quality products, and these products get destroyed by the supply chain handlers without the knowledge of the Amazon FBA. Having said this, you will realize Amazon FBA has the right way of keeping all the tabs of logistics, and this will allow it to keep all records and delivering and acquiring all the ordered items on time. That is, Amazon FBA has inventory management solutions that control the stock and their deliveries. Returns will be straightforward to handle since Amazon has a clear way of doing this.

Amazon Has Got an Accessible Mode of Payment

The method of payment eases the smooth running of the

products. In most cases, you realize that other online trading companies have got restrictions on their terms of payment. More so, this will always destroy the morale of the customers who are very loyal and willing to pay every coin to make purchases. However, this is not in Amazon. Amazon FBA has a transparent mode of payments that allows the customers to make purchases and sells effectively. More so, they accept all types of denominations. For example, if you are in Kenya, and the price of a commodity is 3US dollars, you will pay an amount equivalent to 3 US Dollars by looking at the money exchange rates.

Amazon always has a perfect way of handling its payments in a very convenient manner. And still concentrates much on the way information regarding your payment is dealt with. It can use payment vendors such as PayPal, which will never share financial information with anyone. Before this payment is made, you should notify them about it so that they can create an account. Amazon also accepts E-Check services, which involve paying through your bank account. In this case, you only need to fill in the details where the transfer is moving towards and making sure all account numbers are correct. Again, Amazon accepts the credit cards of all types. That is visa cards, MasterCard, etc. here, you only need to fill in the information required, such as card number, type of cards, expiration date, and even you have to include verification number. Therefore, all these improved the operation of Amazon, leading to an influx of goods and services within the website.

Sellers are getting it more comfortable to sell large volumes within a short period, and this, later on, leads to lots of profit in that financial year. More so, these sellers are left with enough time to handle other profitable duties that might include the sorting of different products for reselling. On the other hand, buyers are not left behind. Buyers will have no hard work in this site since almost all tasks regarding the ordering of the products will be handled by the Amazon. That is, their work is to make a request and wait for the delivery confirmation. Upon reply, the products will just head to the delivery truck and taken for shipment.

Also, this will never take long since their shipping is at least two days. A two-day shipment will allow you to have fresh produce in the case of groceries. Amazon has a clear channel of delivering its message to its customers. As a result of this, many people are turning to it as among the best online trading site. In Amazon, immediately, your product is packed, you will receive a message indicating all the required information. As a consumer, you will go through the information, making a good confirmation about the products you ordered. In case everything is correct, then you will have to make a confirmation message that allows them to load your products on the waiting delivery truck. You will then wait for sometimes mostly two days, but this will always depend on your geographical location.

Therefore, this will leave buyers with much more to save. Again, since delivery time is less, meaning you are getting products when they are still fresh, the quality will be high. Remember, this only applies to products that have shorter lifespans. Quality products in the case of groceries will enable you to consume a healthy related diet, which will later prevent you from any form of health-related complications.

Amazon Has Unlimited Preferences in Terms of Payments

Several websites have listed and stated the types of payments they want, and without this, you will be in great jeopardy. In most cases, the customers, whether buyers or sellers, will find it hard when their preferred mode of payment is not listed. However, this problem is no longer an issue with the Amazon FBA. That is, Amazon has an e-security system such as TRUSTe, which allows the website to have the full trust of the consumers. More so, some payments can be made through PayPal, where the information of the buyer will never be disclosed to anybody. This will results in large sales since consumers can order various products without limitations.

Moreover, you will be able to acquire all the products that you need as much as you have the resources required, such as enough money in your account. After this, all the remaining processes will be handled by the Amazon FBA members who will work tirelessly to deliver your products as soon as possible. You will realize that you are left with enough time to handle other profitable duties. Remember, when we talk about profits, having enough time in business to undertake additional roles gives you much profit.

Provisions of Excellent Products with High Quality

Quality of a product refers to a condition of a product which makes it fit for use and yields the maximum satisfaction expected by the consumer. However, to some people, quality is conformance to standards while others will talk about it being related to value or even that worthiness for your own money. Surprisingly, the quality of the product has been a critical issue since time memorial with the expansion of the online platforms and other online trading websites.

Unfortunately, several vendors are using attractive pictures to lure in the consumers who will end up purchasing all these products. Funny enough, at the buyer level, the quality they expected was not the one being presented to them. That is, the product on display had good qualities as compared to the ones being presented to them. Amazon has come up with strict instructions on how to manage the qualities of products being sold on its websites. At the same time, taking care of the consumer interest regarding the quality they demanded. Therefore, several ways have been put forward to solve this problematic catastrophe concerning the quality of a product.

One way is the introduction of the FBA, which literally means Fulfillment by Amazon. Here, you will realize that all products being offered have to undergo through this system of fulfillment. Therefore, Amazon will only display those items that have passed here. Meaning, they will be of a high standard. Products going through this system will be readily accessible. Hence, this will be reducing the distance between the vendor and the buyer. That is, bridging the gap between the consumer by making sure that the product reaches within a short period. In the end, consuming a high-quality product will lead to much more profit, which will translate to health and other resources.

All in all, making a profit in Amazon is a process that needs time and patience. When you are in a position of managing an online business, you will only need money for starting the business, but this doesn't mean all will go well. However, in Amazon, your chances of getting the worthiness of your money are always high. Therefore, the above reasons plus others, such as convenience, time management, and transparency are some of the solid reasons why people will always opt for Amazon as their favorite choice.

Chapter 3: How Does Amazon FBA Create Financial Freedom

It is always understood that Amazon began as a small and tiny website that mainly concentrated on selling used books. The site started its expansion to an extent causing jitters among the other competitors. To date, Amazon is worth over $605 billion, and with the trend, it might hit a $1 trillion figure in the coming financial year.

Therefore, this implies that it is one of the best sites where we can make more income. There are several ways that we can eventually use to realize our financial freedom within this online platform. In this chapter, we are going to concentrate on several ways you can implement to achieve your financial freedom. Below are the best ways being approved daily as favorite techniques for making financial freedom within the Amazon FBA:

Amazon FBA Allows You to Sell Your Product Using Its Trademark

FBA refers to fulfillment by Amazon, and as a vendor, you will only deliver your product into the Amazon warehouses. Amazon FBA will now take action on your products by paying for shipping fees, especially if you are a prime member of Amazon FBA. However, some people prefer to do the shipping out by themselves to reduce the hefty charges of the Amazon. Fortunately, if you are dealing with a high volume of products, then you need not worry about this since it will be highly beneficial. By selling your product using Amazon FBA, you will be creating a situation where your products reach many people.

Amazon itself has a larger market share, especially across the world. When products get an excellent level of advertisement, it will attract more consumers who will try to make a purchase. At the same time, owing to the respect people have for Amazon, no one will ever doubt its operations. There are other several ways in which you can still make some income in Amazon, but the best one is by becoming a seller. Selling in Amazon has the most excellent opportunity, which will help you manage your ways to financial freedom. Even though selling here proves to be the best, you need to understand or comprehend everything about Amazon FBA.

However, without this, then you might get shocked along the way. Therefore, you need to do proper research on which segment of the market you can get yourself into and start your operations. Due to this, you can start yourself off by using YouTube. In this situation, get those tutorials being displayed there on how to make money on Amazon FBA then note down the key points.

Moreover, you can also do your research by reading several pdf, books, and even newspapers. Again, you should not hesitate to ask the Amazon FBA gurus who have been into this business for long since they are embraced with the rich knowledge about Amazon. Therefore, getting enough information and starting off to sell in the Amazon will slowly create your financial freedom. Remember, financial independence is a process that needs patience, hard work, and courage. More so, it needs time since you cannot just venture into business and get a skyrocket profit.

You Can Create Private Label All of Your Products Within the Amazon

Competitions are everywhere, and in all types of business, we must meet severe or vigorous competitions. Therefore, to avoid this, you can try using your own trademarks within the Amazon FBA. That is, you are registering your products as your own on the Amazon even though this process sometimes is very sophisticated or rather complicated. However, by using your own trademark on Amazon, you will have full control of your products. Therefore, this implies that any bad reviews of your products you can quickly amend it, making sure the customers get the complete satisfaction of your products. In the long run, this will lead to higher purchases as more orders will be realized, thereby leading to a lot of profit in that financial year. As a result, this will translate into financial freedom of the seller. For example, let's say you are dealing with pencils, and you realize that there are lots of negative reviews about the tip of the pens. In this situation, you can go ahead and rectify your product and trademark it again.

Retail Arbitrage

In this category, you realize you will be buying or purchasing at low prices and selling at higher prices. It is always the opposite of private labeling, and some sellers or vendors make their own living from this type. That is, these sellers have created themselves a lucrative niche that only benefits them alone.

It is good to note that sellers who undertake this type of retailing always try as much as possible to avoid the shipping fee. In a case where they are not prime members of Amazon, they will prevent instances of importing products for resell and just make a regular purchase from the nearest locations. Thus, this will save them time, money, and other resources such as fuel and much more.

In most cases, you will realize that places like Walmart, which offer the best deals with lower buying prices will record an impulse buying. All these products will end up on the Amazon website, where they will fetch higher prices leading to more financial gains. All these, in the end, will create a passive income leading to financial freedom. However, you should note down the precautions of starting this business since it is not always an easier gig. That is, it needs a lot of time to start realizing much gains from this. Therefore, as long as you have passion, you will be in a position to deliver your promise to your customers. Also, you will be able to create more sales, which will later translate into a lot of profits leading to financial freedom.

You Can Work as Their Delivery Associate

Amazon attracts many sellers and buyers all over the years. It has been estimated to have over 150 million online sellers and buyers who log in to this website for various reasons. As a result, it will have to provide as many products as possible to maintain all these people. However, the only way to manage these is to have a clear aspect of the products being brought in by the sellers. Thus, for quick handling of all these products, Amazon has to employ as many as possible people who will work in their various fulfillment centers, delivery stations, sorting stations, customer service centers, pick points, and even Prime Now Locations. In this scenario, you will either be a full time or part-time depending on your available time. Therefore within some periods, you will realize some financial gains which might, in the end, result in financial freedom.

You Can Be an Amazon Affiliate

An Amazon FBA business model always leverages the principles of warehousing and fulfillment functions. This will always make it easier for you to become an affiliate in this business. Therefore, when you become an affiliate, you will be entitled to some commissions. That is the moment you make a referral to customers who, in the end, might purchase our products. In this case, you will be making a double profit. However, being an affiliate needs time and patience. More so, to realize some excellent deals in terms of incomes within that financial year, you will have to be patient and vigorous while referring customers. In this business of referral, you will have to work extra hard so that you increase your commissions too. The earned commission will increase your gains within the Amazon, which will lead to financial freedom.

You Can Sell Handmade to Amazon

Amazon, most of the time, will not accept the handmade

items from people. Remember, from the beginning Amazon was only selling used books and later on changed to general products. However, if you have perfect skills in making the handmade products, you will only apply to Amazon so that you will be allowed to sell on their website. There are handmade items that you can always trade on this website, such as bags, jewelry, and much more. Even though these products will face stiff competition from the various sectors such as eBay and Etsy, in Amazon, if allowed, you will make a lot of money. That is, on this website, we have over 150 million people who always log in to either purchase or sell. At the same time, regarding the flexing muscle of the Amazon, you will realize your product catches enough traffic, which will lead to more sales.

More so, remember, Amazon will always opt for advertising your products since there is a small fee it still charges when the products have been sold. However, how does this create a financial freedom status quo? It is very simple. When you make hand made products within your comfort zone, you will never be charged shipping fee since you will just deliver them by yourself to their premises. Secondly, handmade items don't require hefty charges while handling, and because of that, you will never pay more in this situation. Therefore, you need to realize that by paying less in terms of charges and generating huge sales, you will end up accomplishing more incomes, which will translate to passive income. Again, raw inputs for making handmade products are readily available at a lower price. As a result, you will be creating a situation of financial freedom.

Merits and Demerits of Amazon FBA

The Merits of Amazon FBA

Fulfillment by Amazon is the most attractive online platform where sellers and buyers throng to have their products sold or acquired. There are many reasons why we would prefer using Amazon FBA and no other online platforms. Below are some of the outstanding merits of Amazon FBA:

Payment Preferences Are unlimited

In most cases, buyers or sellers will find it hard when their preferred mode of payment is not listed. However, this problem is no longer an issue with the Amazon FBA. That is, Amazon has an e-security system such as TRUSTe, which allows the website to have the full trust of the consumers. This will results in large sales since consumers can order various products without limitations. More so, you will be in a position to acquire all the products that you need as long as you have the resources required. Mode of payment will never be an issue, and payments of the products can be made by a click from the button. After this, all the remaining processes will be handled by the Amazon FBA members who will work tirelessly to deliver your products as soon as possible.

High Product Quality

The product quality has been an issue since time memorial with the expansion of the online platforms. Unfortunately, various sellers are using pleasing and attractive pictures to attract customers who will end up buying goods and services. Sadly, at the consumer level, the quality standard being presented to them was not the one within the display. Amazon has come up with guidelines on how to control the quality of its products. One way is the introduction of the FBA, which literally means Fulfillment by Amazon. In this case, you will realize all goods and services being offered have to undergo through this model of fulfillment.

The site will only display those items that have passed here. Meaning, they will be of a high standard. Goods passing through this model will be readily accessible, and this will also reduce the distance between the seller and the consumer. That is, bridging the gap between the consumer by making sure that the product reaches within a short period. In the end, this increases the quality of the product since the customer can get the product when it is still fresh, especially in the case of groceries and other fresh produce.

Powerful Logistics Within the Website

The logistics used here by several online traders are just a big mess, unlike to what Amazon FBA is offering. That is cases of poor delivery, barring of websites, and much more is becoming a significant challenge in the online trade. Sometimes, the deliveries end up missing, and that means a consumer can wait for quite some time to get the ordered item. However, at that time may be the use of that product is no more. Sometimes, the packaging becomes so poor that the quality of the product reduces along the supply chain. That is, here comes a case where the seller gave out high-quality products, and these products get destroyed by those handling.

The Amazon FBA has the right way of keeping all the tabs of logistics, and this will allow it to keep all records and delivering and acquiring all the ordered items on time. That is, Amazon FBA has inventory management solutions that control the stock, their deliveries, and much more. Cases of returns are never an issue with the outlaid quality checks up through the FBA. More so, this online platform has a hassle-free returns policy that enables it, buyers, and sellers to have a smooth running of the website. That is, in case of anything, then returning items will be much easier. Logistics also help to prevent any risk related to missing of the products, invoices, and receipts of payments. This will create a conducive environment for the working of online trade.

Delivery Time Is Apparent

Amazon has a clear channel of delivering its message to its customers. As a result of this, many people are turning to it as among the best online trading site. In Amazon, immediately, your product is packed, you will receive a message indicating all the required information. As a consumer, you will go through the information, making a good confirmation about the products you ordered. In case everything is correct, then you will have to make a confirmation message which allows them to load your products on the waiting delivery truck. You will then wait for sometimes mostly two days, but this will always depend on your geographical location.

Availability of Shipping Discounts

Prime members of Amazon boast of having this discount. And because of this, it is forming part of the advantage as to why most people would prefer it. On most occasions, most sellers or buyers will prefer online trading sites where they are being given incentives such as discounts; however little it might be. Since Amazon commands a huge and enormous share of the market, it is shipping lots of products daily. As a result, there is a quick need for a convenient mode of transport. Therefore, Amazon made a business agreement with large shipping carriers who later on give them some steep discounts. However, all these discounts are passed to both sellers and buyers. That is, to the vendors, they are given a reduced shipping fee, especially when they are their products to the Amazon warehouse. However, customers, in most cases, don't pay the delivery fee since shipping is free.

Management of Returns

The most advantage of this platform is its ability to manage returns, especially when the products are faulty. More so, this also applies when the products are not up to the standard of the expectations of the customers. In most sites, this will be hell. However, in Amazon, it will never take long for the return process to be achieved.

Customer Service Management

Amazon FBA offers an endless customer care service through phone calls chats and even emails. As a result, the customers will never have anxiety about anything relating to the products within the Amazon.

Excellent Unlimited Storage Space

The moment you are using FBA, you should not worry about

the storage. More so, you should not worry about the warehouse since Amazon FBA handles this free of charge.

Demerits of Amazon (FBA)

Amazon FBA is regarded as a selling machine that can make more profits within a short period. However, there are some drawbacks those who are involved should be aware comprehend. Below are some of the worst disadvantages of Amazon FBA:

Fulfillment by Amazon Costs Money.

This platform tends to charge a double fee sometimes. That is fulfillment and storage fees. As a result, you have to closely monitor the movement of your products so that you minimize the charges such as storage fees. At the same time, you want to make sure that you will still have a profit even after paying storage fees and fulfillment fees.

Long-Term Storage Fees.

The work of Amazon FBA is to make sure that all products are sold since it also has a partial share in your inventory. However, here comes a situation where your stocks are overstaying in the warehouse. A situation like this will lead to excess fees being charged. In most cases, Amazon FBA will start charging more fees when the products stay for over six months without being purchased by the customers.

You May See More Returns.

Returns in all business are not good news at all. In a situation where the system provides hassle-free return policies, many customers will tend to return more products with the reason of faultiness. Again, in a case where the returns process is free, many customers will have impulse buying to test some which they will later return.

Product Prep Can Be Stressful.

This online trade platform has one of the complicated and most strict guidelines on how to ship and prepare items. In this case, products have to be entered correctly into the database of the Amazon. Again, these products must be correctly labeled and then delivered to the right warehouse. However, it will be difficult to perform all these, especially when you are a newbie in this business.

Complicated Tracking Process of the Inventory

Sometimes there are difficulties in managing a tracking process of your stocks. Sometimes, you are running out of products within the warehouse, and no useful information is forthcoming. However, in some situations, you will not even be aware of what you need to order or even what is no longer selling within the market. Sadly, because of this, you will find it challenging to stay on top with the rest of your competitors. At the same time, knowing the trending products will be another weird situation. More so, selling products using various channels will make it difficult to track the products.

Chapter 4: Details on How to Choose Profitable Product (Private Label)

There are a different set of guidelines that are used when choosing a profitable product on Amazon FBA. Most people talk about research when they think of any business with potential success. Conducting market research for your products should indeed be an essential part of the company. Right products usually have a very substantial demand in the market. This ever-growing demand if not met the supply can be said to below. When you introduce the right products to the market, then your business will grow as profits increase. Time should be allocated to researching different products. Therefore product selection mostly depends on its quality and the level of customers' satisfaction. Be keen on finding the detailed procedure of appraisal that maximizes one's success with the product. All business people strive to make profit thud different criteria used to find profitable products.

The Rank of Sales

It is especially essential for sellers who intend to sell multiple units per day. Sales rank usually varies by category. There are categories that rank more depending on the demand, supply, and quality of the product. Always try to be under 20,000; that way, you will be in a safe spot that is not too high or too low. But the general rule used by many usually is under 50,000. A good example is if you happen to have popular category products and you are under 20,000, there is a high chance that you will sell more. For this reason, therefore, always focus on overall category rank. Do not be just glued to a sob category rank. He also advised that category ranks always changes, so be up to date and make necessary adjustments at any particular time.

Profit for Each Sale

There are different products with different qualities. It is, therefore, important to determine which product will yield more profit per sale. Most Sellers often focus on ROI when choosing products. This way, they can determine the profit per product sold. While one may be tempted to focus on achieving 100%, it is safe to start looking at a minimum of 30%. To achieve much profit as desired you can use a combination of profit sales per year and ROI.

For example, if your profit is a minimum 10$ per sale that would be ideal. It will give you room to grow when other sellers decide to drop their prices to compete in the market. When your profit is less, let's say 6$ or lower than that you may lose all your profits. Especially is someone who decides to drop their prices. The only way to determine your cash reserves is through the use of profit per sale and ROI. But for those who are rich in terms of cash ROI, thus will be less of a factor. In this scenario, therefore, the focus will be on profit per sale.

Product Size

Amazon products vary greatly, even products that serve the same purpose. They are grouped into two major categories; 'Oversize' and 'standard.' The choice is yours, depending on your desired outcome and goal. Some are just starting up and those who have experience in trading with Amazon. For those who are just doing their preparations and starting, then strive to stick to smaller items. It may not just because they are small in size and usually cheaper. They are straightforward to handle; you will use a cheaper amount during shipment to Amazon. Their storage costs are often less compared to their larger items' counterparts.

There are some situations where you need to store them in your house for a while. In this case, therefore, you will use less space and store more. It means that the returns will also be straightforward to deal with. Larger products may need special equipment during handling. They can take larger storage space, and you can be limited in terms of the number you can ship at ago. The Shipment fees will also be costly. The size of the product also determines the final number of sales. Smaller size products sell more and most often can be ordered many at ago. It is because even customers also do not mind shipment charges of smaller products. Larger products most often realize fewer orders; standard category products are the best choice for those new trading with Amazon.

Gated Brands

While many people are familiar with the term Brand and Categories, the term gated may not be familiar to many. Most Amazon categories and brands are usually gated. It means that one cannot sell the products unless they get permission from Amazon. Before you purchase a stock be keen on restrictions and do your research well. You won't need to purchase a stock that you will not be able to sell or resell. For new sellers, always focus on just the products you can sell. Make this work first before trying to add more products with restrictions. You can achieve this by downloading the Amazon seller app from the play store. Alternatively, you can click on 'Add product' in Seller central to justify if there is an existing restriction. Once you have verified all these, then you can now comfortable purchase your stock and start selling. You can also open up a different category of products. You will find many services available that will guide you through all the steps to get ungated products in multiple categories. Even with the most difficult categories or restricted categories, it is still possible to get ungated products. You can also consider taking an online course on Getting Ungated products on Amazon.

Brands That Are High Risk

These kinds of brands refer to the brands that Amazon allows you to sell them to clients, but the brand owner does not allow you to sell them. New sellers have experiences suspension for selling these kinds of brands. Because brand owners do not allow the sellers to sell them, the brand owners will, therefore, take action to stop the sellers from s4elling the product because the sellers do not have their permission. In this scenario, brand owners usually take legal action and sometimes policy warning though Amazon. You should be very keen on suspension. This is because once you are suspended, chances of you getting your account back are very slim.

Conduct a lot of research on the product you are selling. If you notice that it may not be safe or you do not have permission from the brand owner the sell it, simply remove it from the list. Thus will not only make you avoid the legal action but help you be safe and thus not face suspension. Be sure that all the products you are selling are not gated, and you are free to sell them. Do not risk your account because of one particular brand.

Value of the Product

Different products have different values, even the product that is the same in terms of functionality. For you to stay safe and put, have a product that you can comfortably write off when required to do so. There are many situations where a customer can return a product; this may because they are not satisfied with the product or damages during shipment. In this scenario, you may have to dispose of the product if it is damaged and cannot be repaired. If the disposal may bring your business down, then you are not in a safety net.

The ideal product value in the market you should be focusing on is $10-$50 that has a price range of $10-$20.As you grow in terms of experience, then you will be able to aim for higher-end products. Try as much as possible not to go beyond $100, as this may cause you to lose that you will be unable to recover. Some products will realize an increase in value once their manufacturing stops. If you buy such products, you will have a built-in safety measure whenever the product does not sell as anticipated. You will not be worried even if you leave it at the FBA warehouse because it will eventually sell for a better profit.

The Return Rate of the Product

There is a product that usually has a return rate or 10% and more. You should avoid these products at all costs. This is because the return rate will cost you money. It is thus like an expense on your part. So the higher the return rate is, the higher the chances of you losing your money. There are products that once they are returned, cannot resell them or fix them and has to dispose of them. It will be due to the type of packaging of the products. Where customers have to damage the package before getting hold of the product and looking at the product.

For this reason, you will dispose of the product or sell it at a ridiculously low price. Before you choose a product, check the product review and customers' comments. If possible, any product with less than a 4star rating should be a no-no. Also, avoid much more complex products as their return rate is usually very high. Be careful not to spend money on returns. This may damage your business. Once customers return the product, they usually give it a poor rating and sometimes mean comments. In this case, also prior research is necessary to enable you not to make the wrong decision. To avoid expenses arriving from high return rate always aim at products which are tough and well packaged. These products are not easily damaged in the FBA warehouse or even during shipment or transit to customers. If you do these, you will realize fewer complaints about customers and thus less negative feedback.

Product Price History

This can also relate to the buying price of the particular product. For example, a product can sell on Amazon for $30, and you find out from the Keepa charts that the amount is also the normal selling price. Be keen on Keepa and Carmel charts on the selling price of the product. If the price you are selling it for is the same market price, then you may risk sitting in added stock. This is because customers may not see the need for buying online and paying the extra delivery fees if the market value is the same.

Aim at products that you can sell at an average price and still break even and earn some profits. These kinds of products will help you increase sales, thus making more profit. Price history can also ensure customer retention since most customers always refer to the products they use to their friends' colleagues and social media for influencers. Do not be a seller who is attracted by a temporary price increase as this is luring and makes you feel you will make more profit.

In reality, however, when you list the product in the market, the price will have dropped or returned to normal, and you will realize a loss. For those not familiar with Keepa chart, it is an extension of chrome that directly loads the Amazon listing page. Keepa provides a lot of insight with regards to the product's sale history and pricing. For example, if the product is a new FBA product then consider removing the term 'used' and instead ensure that the words like 'New,' 'Sales Rank,' and 'Amazon' are clearly showing. For view purposes, you can use the last three months, but keep in mind that potential clients have access to the entire life span of the products so as to get additional insights.

Amazon Categories

You should also consider the category you want to invest in. This is by keeping in mind the issues already discussed, like:

the return rate, the value of the product and size. To be safe, some people start with Toys. This is because toys in most cases have the lowest return rate compared to top other products; they are also simple and not large or bulky. Other people, however, consider starting with office products or home and kitchen. This is because these products have high demand value and just like toys, low return rates.

Electronics are avoided by most sellers starting up because they have a high return rate, thus result in losses. You may realize that the products you are passionate about may not be the most viable product to trade-in. Since it is business and the main aim is profit-making, then your passion can be an added advantage if you use it in your favor. This is because you can feel the products and spot good, better deals that can realize more profit. Choose a category that best suits you and your business. Also, do not be in a rush to choose any category just because you think it can give you much profit in a short time.

How to Harmonize Product with Brand

This issue always appeals to many, and the feedback sometimes is very puzzle. The relationship between a brand and a product is very crucial as this can positively influence customer retention. While some customers are more concerned with the products they are purchasing, most customers are obsessed with brands. The bigger the brand, the higher the market value of their products. Some companies have known this trick and manufacture the same products and do some slight alteration in their appearance so as to differentiate between the brands. Most consumers do not see this trick yet, so they choose to go for the brand they are used to.

Always identify the right product for the consumers. This is the necessary foundation for a successful private level business. Once you get the right product ideas, do research on well-known brands. You can incorporate one of their production, and in the description, the box makes sure that the brand you are interested in appears. By this, you can even sell products not associated with the brand since the consumer may start relating it to the other. But be careful not to lie that a product falls in the category of a brand it does not.

You can also develop a product idealist who is well suited for the particular private level business you are engaged in. You do not need perfect brands or perfect products. You only need to conduct enough research and come up with amazing sales strategies. You can use Amazon's best sellers list to find out the products doing well as well as brands concerned from there, pick related products from most preferred brands, and incorporate them. You can also use the creative brainstorming unstructured method. By this, it means that you put everything (products and brands) you touch in two days. Then you can now research the products and brands. You can get more ideas from advertisements, commercials, and customer feedback on product reviews. The most important thing is, the best product sells more, and a brand can act as a marketing tool. Also, brands play a very significant role in introducing a new product on the market.

Chapter 5: Define the Product for Sale in Retail Arbitrage

Amazon is attracting a large number of people daily. So far, so good, people are shifting their online trade towards Amazon. With the lots of profits being generated, both sellers and consumers are looking for ways to seek financial freedom from the platform. Therefore, because of this, Amazon has created a pathway that everyone can follow to realize their ultimate dreams of being part and parcel of the eCommerce. That is, you can be a prime member of Amazon through retail arbitrage, as a wholesaler, and much more.

However, there are some security policies that you have to satisfy to consider yourself as a retail arbitrage partner. These conditions include the types of goods and services you offer, the manufacturers of those products, warranties of the products you want to offer, and working relationships between the manufacturers or your suppliers and the Amazon. Fortunately, Amazon will dwell much on the invoices of your products, and this will be through the trusted suppliers of the manufacturers. Remember, you should take note that Amazon is the leading online trading platform that works best to eliminate any scam in the online trading business. Therefore, they will do anything possible to remove it. One way is to seek the authenticity of your products. That being said, you need to know the real definition of retail arbitrage before getting back on our main objective of the chapter.

Retail arbitrage refers to a situation where you purchase your products through a retail store and resell it. That is when buying products and looking the ways to make it more attractive then reselling it at higher prices. However, you can also purchase goods from other online trading websites and sell them in Amazon after adding some small price on top. A good example is when you buy some clearance items from different online platforms such as Target, Ross, Big Lots, and even Close Out Sales and going ahead to list them for sale on Amazon. Sometimes they send these products to the FBA so that they can fetch higher prices. However, this always comes with challenges and risks which involve issues of warranties since most of them don't honor warranties. Therefore this implies that the moment you do retail and the product is not worth the expectations of the buyers, you, as a retailer, might plunge into a hell of losses. Sadly, this is a situation that the Amazon platform will struggle as hard as possible to avoid.

More so, you can also say that retail arbitrage is a practice of spotting a gap and using the different prices of the same products to strike an advantage. That is when you strike an effective combination of the right deals, which lead to more profit upon the imbalance prices in different online sites. In this case, your main aim is to take advantage of the prices being offered in other online trading sites. From a quick understanding, you can use this illustration. Assume a particular product is marked at a price of 24US Dollars on eBay, while the same product will cost the consumers about 28US Dollars on Amazon. In this case, you can chip in and take that advantage. In this situation, you will manage to have a profit of 4US Dollars.

Products Allowed in Amazon

Many brand owners are on the lookout when it comes to goods and services being uploaded on the website for a resell. This has led to greater restrictions by the Amazon to those indulging into retail arbitrage. Below are products that you will find it easy to work with as far as you are an Amazon prime member through retail arbitrage.

Avoid Selling Counterfeit Products.

In this situation, any form of counterfeit will be met with severe penalties, which might even lead to the closure of your account. Always prefer getting products through the trusted distributors of the manufacturing companies. Through this, you will be in a position to have enough proof of your products. That is, your authentic deals will never be in doubt.

Try as Hard as Possible to Sell New Products

When I talk about new products, I refer to those items that have not been used anywhere. That is, your first consumer will be the first person to use that item. Remember, your product should have a warranty, especially from the manufacturers themselves. By providing this, you will be in a position to prove beyond doubts that our product is original, and no one should doubt it under any circumstances.

Avoid Big Brands Such as Nike, Apple and Much More

Big brands are known for killing the morale of those venturing into retail arbitrage. This is because they have high standards when it comes to their policies. Again, you will never make a profit in Amazon using these brands. In most situations, big brand companies tend not to allow any form of third-party reselling, especially on an online platform such as Amazon. That is, the moment you will try this, you might get up, making more losses as compared to what you expected.

An Apple product such as phones might fetch higher prices on all sites. On the other hand, Amazon prefers trading on items with lower prices to attract many customers. What you need to understand here is the fact that Amazon is doing business. Any form of marketing is supposed to yield a maximum profit at the end of every financial year. All these will depend on the volume of products sold.

Therefore, the only way to achieve a larger volume is to concentrate on items with lower prices, which will end up attracting a large number of consumers. This will later reflect on the accrued profits made at the end. Still, on this, Apple and other big-brand companies can shut down all the retailers using their products in different online trade. Unfortunately, especially when you are never part and parcel of their distributing stream.

You Must Use Your Trademark on Different Goods You Are Retailing

As far as selling on someone else trademark might leads to maximum profit, Amazon tends not allowing that. According to their argument, when you do this, you will be breaching the rules and regulations explained in this site. Remember, Amazon is defending and protecting its image, and because of this, it has attracted almost over 150 million people. It protects the buyer, seller, and even the manufactures. In a situation where you will be found illegally using a trademark that is not yours, then you will have to explain it in detail. This might even lead to the closure of your account.

You Can Only Sell Post Priced Items

Amazon will never accept any item with pre-priced labels. This is well explained in their policies and regulations. Below are some of the products you are not supposed to operate on:

- Floating or sky lanterns
- Gift cards, stored valued instruments and other gift certificates
- Vehicle tires too are not allowed
- Alcohol beverages and non-alcoholic beers
- Avoid those products with those unaccepted marketing materials such as price tags, pamphlets, and other non-Amazon stickers and logos.

Don't Sell Used Conditioned Products

Amazon will not allow you to resell products that already have been used; however, how good condition they might look. These include the following:

Defective or Damaged Units

Loose and default packaged batteries. Items such as phones with removable batteries might be a threat to quality standards.

Various products that require preparation but has not met the packaging and prep requirements of the FBA. These products might be in poor condition since the Amazon community might even fail to understand the quality of the product packaged.

Registered Products with the AMAZON

Registered products consist of labels, logos that indicate that Amazon is part and parcel of the product you are retailing. Remember, Amazon can cancel any trade of items that are not correctly registered with Amazon. Again, some items do not correspond to the ones that were registered.

All Products Being Sold Must Comply with the Policies.

As a retailer, agreements are binding you together with the Amazon that is well explained in your FBA account. Those binding agreements should be taken care of and implemented all the time. Failure to that, then your business with Amazon will just come to an end.

Don't Sell Duplicated or Reproduced Items.

Any product which is replicated or reproduced in any manner will not be accepted. This also applies to the ones that a retailer might decide to duplicate. A good example is where a seller is creating several copies of a book that does not belong to them to resell it. More so, this is not acceptable by the publishers at all and always leads to severe penalties.

You Can Only Sell Suitable Products

There are some products that Amazon considers as not suitable at all. These products might include vehicle tires, replicated items, and much more.

Nevertheless, selling and buying on Amazon has been a successful journey that everyone wants to start. Choosing the best product without restrictions under the laws governing the Amazon's products will be the best path to follow. Everyone can make a trial in Amazon retail as long as you have an account. The only way to go about it is to make sure that you are making great impressions on the following areas:

- Product weight and dimensions should be appealing
- Beautiful and attractive colors, sizes, etc.
- Promised warranty information with all the required details
- Product specs sheets
- Installation guidelines in case of products such as machines and so on.

Therefore when you need to know in business, you have to have a passion for you to operate and realize a long-term benefit. During this time, your primary focus should be the ability to offer more products with attractive buying prices. In the end, this will attract many customers leading to more sales, which later on reflect on the profits. Be on the lookout and make the best in terms of selling. That is, being on top of the best seller ranking will enable you to attract more customers, which again will lead to more sales leading to excess profits.

However, for you to realize more sales, you must consider the site and sight recognition of your products. If you invest entirely in this technique, you will create a proper brand recognition which will make it easier for the buyers to locate you wherever you are. In this situation, you have to prefer tag lines, themes, logos, etc. another way to increase your gains here is to look for ways to become an affiliate member of Amazon. This will help you to earn more commissions while at the same time giving you enough time to advertise your products. That is, being an affiliate member will make you get in touch with numerous customers, and using the first pledge, you will be able to realize more sales. In the end, you will be making lots of profits.

Chapter 6: Techniques to Help You Make a Powerful and Perfect Launch of a Product

Successful entrepreneurs usually are very keen when launching a new product on the market. Product launch if not done well, can make a company lose profits. It's no wonder why most businesses, both existing and new, are always excited when they are launching a new product. It can be a new product or an improved version of the product that already exists. New product launch often sparks the enthusiasm of potential profit by the entrepreneurs. Entrepreneurs need to know that there are various techniques that they need to use before launching the product in the market.

Evaluation of Market and Product

Assessment can be done before launching a product. It is not possible to gauge how the product will be received in the market once it's launched. You can do some introspective study and analyze the market needs. From there, you can also evaluate your firm. Confirm your company's readiness before you start publicizing the new product. By doing this, you can answer questions like if the company is ready to support overnight and fast growth in case that will be the result.

All product launches aimed at making profits if that happens bigger than your expectations; you need to be able to meet the increased demand. Have a clear protocol when it comes to customer care. It may include customer queries, returns, complains, and reviews. Have all those resources needed in place to enable you to carry out a perfect launch effectively. Ensure that the product you are launching has been tested, and it will serve the purpose it is intended. You can select a few people and do some testing to get their feedback and recommendations.

Do not ignore harmful products as they help in avoiding the potential risk that may put your business to peril. Evaluation of the market comes by analyzing the report from market research. Adequate market research provides vital information that will, in turn, direct the product launch. The report also helps you identify the right market for the product. As much as market research is time-consuming, it should never be overlooked. Market research helps you know your strengths and potential threats. You can list your competitors at this point and note what makes your product different.

Customer Involvement

Customers are the consumers of the product. They will give you the best insights because they are the actual users of the product. Do not just rely on data from a previous feasibility study. If it is possible, engage them and talk to them directly. Know their specific needs and convince them you are the best in the market. It is merely convincing them that by choosing your product, they have made the best choice. They will give you candid answers on what they think. The truth is customers offer abundant resources that can help in the modification of features. Persuading them does not mean you do let them speak their mind; it is more of convincing them to use the product without forcing them. You need to use open-ended questions when interacting with customers that way; you will get their honest feedback. Involving customers help build a service care environment, and this will improve customer satisfaction once the launch is done.

Ideas Validation

Information gathered should be used to validate one's ideas. The validation process usually involves letting real users test your product. Some entrepreneurs call it going pubic early to determine whether you are on the right path. Avoiding using real users for the test can be compared to shooting with a blindfold. You can do this using a few trusted friends, new users, or power users who can give honest feedback. This will help you find out whether they see the value of the product or if they appreciate it. It is like watching people react to your ideas. It can offer a projection of what to expect after the product has been launched in the market.

Build Your Audience and Community

There are billions of internet users every day. This means that there is a high chance that tons of people will want to purchase your product. Find a way of networking with these people early. Be active in social media, start a blog, or a website. It will help you reach most of your potential customers. If they get to know you and what you do, they will take a keen interest in the particular project you are launching. If you wait until the starting day, some may not respond. You can even create count day to product launch give them an overview of what the product is. An audience can be built around a brand or product before the launch date.

Use Amazon Formula for Writing a Mock Press Release

Press coverage has led to a successful launch of so many products. It can lead to a massive multiplier of product success. Most entrepreneurs, however, do not want to risk involving journalists in their product launch, especially new products. You need to understand that just like customers are interested in product journalists are interested in a story. Show them how useful your product is and how it will get people excited. Do not hide any details.

Amazon also believes in the power of writing a press release before the product launch. Once you create a spreadsheet, write target blogs and publications, you intend to reach out. Pick the reporters who are most likely to write about what product you will be launching. Research on similar products they have covered and how successful the outcomes were. Connect also with other supplementary press partners and companies. Look for influencers with a big following who are most likely to review your product.

Improve Your Organic Visibility

This mostly involves making good use of your SEO. Make sure is it on point. If you position your website thoroughly on the search engines, you will have a base of traffic that enables you to communicate new and upcoming products. This will be easier than starting from square one. Ensure that your users are given useful and relevant information. Use the right keywords that are not misleading or vague. Think about how a new user is likely to search for the product and use those keywords. Remember, also, that users often see meta descriptions regarding website summary on search engines. Sometimes Google will ignore the narrative and show only the first line of the page. So to be safe, make sure your opening line is up to scratch. Write the most important things you need your customers to know in the first paragraph. If they do not find it relevant, they may never proceed to the next section.

The product launch will be realized if you follow the discussed strategies but do not be limited. This is because the product launch needs a lot of preparation and planning. So it is essential to take your time before rushing to the market. Know your target audience. This will help you understand the best way to communicate top them as well as during selection for product testing.

Various Promotions Leading to Sales

As an entrepreneur, you may launch a product in the market, it is very high, but you are not realizing good sales as expected. When this happens, you may wonder what is going wrong. This is where promotion comes in. Advertising can be useful even in future expansions and the general prosperity of the company. Marketing and promotions go together as their aim is to increase sales. Your product will determine the type of advertising you will adapt depending on your goal. In this chapter, however, we will discuss five promotion ideas that can be used to realize sales.

Promotions induce traffic of customers over a short period of time. It is, therefore, used to attract customers away from the competitor. This is because once they try the product, they may like it and switch from what they usually buy. It has also created upselling when a customer is persuaded to buy an expensive product.

Flash Sales

This has been one of the oldest tricks that are still effective and practiced today. Flash sale allows customers to save money if they can act fast. For instance, you can offer an excellent deal on Friday or Wednesday or any other day you choose. Flash sales attract new customers and retain old customers. It can shorten the sales cycle and give a chance to those who have not tested the product to check it. With the flash sale, the business will realize a fast infusion of cash. This can help boost revenue, especially during the slow time of the year. Flash sale creates urgency but keeps promo codes away from coupons sites. You can promote flash sales in advance to let customers know.

Buy A Product Get One Free

If you have ever come across this, then there is a high chance it was on promotion. It can be the same product or a different product altogether. Most people understand the meaning of free. Consumers are more attracted to free stuff than discounts, and they will always go for the one offered for free. Offering a free product when one buys another can help bring in new customers. You can partner with another company or use your product. This promotion is useful because it introduces a customer to the product that in a normal circumstance, they would not have bought.

Coupons and Discount with Purchase

Tickets can be offered or a gift card with a purchase. The customer will get an opportunity to save, thus buys more, and the entrepreneur will realize more sales. Always be keen and ensure that the discount still gives room for profit margin. When offering discounts, you can use the rule of 100. For instance, for products costing more than $100, a dollar amount will be more appealing. For example, you can offer a discount of $20 for a $200 purchase.

Recurring Sales

Customers have been known for waiting for recurring sales that have been offered in the past. You can develop an anniversary sale that way every year when that time reaches you have enough stock of demand to meet supply. It can also be a monthly offer; this means you do not make sales a one-time thing. Recurring transactions will create the consistency that every business needs. This can even help in sales figures comparison.

Tripwire

Prospective customers may not be able to understand you, trust you, or like you. They can only achieve this if they get to experience your products. Tripwire's offer is usually lower in terms of cost and provides a small risk that a prospective customer may not hesitate to buy. Tripwire can be in the form of a book, product trial sample or online course that shows what the company offer and the features of the product. It is something worth investing in. For instance, if a customer spends thirty minutes watching a video about the product, it is most likely that they will not hesitate to buy the product.

Promotions are often used by companies to increase sales in a short time frame to gain market share and sales volume. Most companies have also used promotions as completion strategies to compete with their counterparts. Advertising often succeeds in increasing sales volume over a short span. It does not, however, build brand loyalty and identity. Some companies use various promotions to get rid of old inventory without running at a loss.

Competition for customer attention has increased over the years. This is because many new products are introduced each year. Marketers, therefore, often invest in various promotions strategies to attract more customers. The promotions have multiple benefits from boosting sales short-term to influencing positive online reviews and thus repeat purchases in the future. A customer today prefers full product experience as this will match their standards when it comes to product quality. They will, therefore, prefer relevant offers and will not hesitate to try them during the promotion period. By doing this, they will be able to decide whether or not they want to stick with you, but there is a high chance they will.

Chapter 7: Reasons Why People Prefer Amazon Retail Arbitrage Instead of Private Label Method

Retail arbitrage refers to the process that involves buying products from companies that are closing their business and are disposing of their assets to settle their dues. It is the use of the internet to search for products and buy low mat prices. Then they will have the sole intention of selling them at a higher price with the end goal of making a profit. At this point, usually, and one can acquire goods at rather low prices than the retail prices on Amazon.

The advantage of this kind of sourcing is that very few people are in a position to acquire goods from dissolving companies and are not reluctant to pay the stated retail prices. This method is even better because one does not require a website to be able to sell the products. As an entrepreneur, you can maximize the advantage of the platform that Amazon offers as a business medium. This is because the startup cost is very minimal as all you need is your complete list of goods or the contents in stock.

On Amazon, This Is How the Process Works:

- Look for the products from the different stores, buy them, and have them delivered to Amazon stores.
- Amazon will then do the packaging of the products after they have received them.
- When an order is placed, Amazon takes the responsibility of delivering the product to the customer
- Amazon then facilitates your payment through your specified payment options by crediting your payment to your account.

The Merits of Retail Arbitrage Which Makes It Preferable

Capital

The cost of venturing into this business is very low, as the high cost is the purchase of the goods. The other investment is simple as one only requires as software, paying for an account, and the presenting costs.

The model only requires you to identify a reasonable offer, bargain for the best prices, make the purchase, and have the goods delivered to their warehouse. At infrequent times will one require to create an inventory as Amazon will do it for them. There is also no need for marketing and advertisement as the markets for the products are often ready. The possibility of trading in different products is dependent on one's ability to identify and source various products for trade.

Profit-Making Period

The end goal of starting a business has been able to make profits. In retail arbitrage, this is a high possibility compared to making your own private venture, which can also be achieved within a very short period of trading.

Reduced Volatility

In retail arbitrage, in the chance of making a mistake in regard to the choice of goods purchased, this is only capable of affecting a small percentage of your business and rarely the whole business. This provides the businessman with the opportunity to purchase a different product and progressing with the new brands as compared to private labels where one is limited to the products produced.

Retail Arbitrage on Amazon

Taking advantage of the huge network provided by Amazon and beginning to make money involves very simple steps.

Amazon runs an application referred to as Fulfillment by Amazon (FBA) that allows tradesmen to store their goods with Amazon up to the time they are sold. This only happens at a small cost and saves the business person the hustle of looking for a store at an added cost.

When a client orders for an item, Amazon packages it, and it's directly shipped to the client. In case of a return, Amazon still takes care of that. However, the charges incurred by the business person in using FBA are dependent on the number of items they are selling, their duration of storage in their warehouse, item size, and the paying plan, be it monthly or on a single item differently.

Reasons Why People Prefer Amazon Retail Arbitrage

In the ranking of popular companies in the United States, Amazon has been able to be among the top five companies holding position four while in the world, the company managed to be top ten been ranked as number ten. This in itself shows the number of audiences the company site reaches not only in Seattle, where it is based but in the world in general. The company has diversified its business ventures while maintaining the retail business as its core, thus allowing everyone in the desire to make an extra income be it for businessmen or part-time workers.

Retail arbitrage provides an option that is faster, effortless with minimal risks involved in starting up a business if you could compare on venturing on your private label. For the sole reason that as a business person you are trading in goods that have been in existence in the market, there will be little or no investment required to be made in your attempt to convince or market the products because already the market is available. With the available ready market, business runs as soon as you get to list your products on Amazon compared to the grace period that a private label would require to advertise and market to be able to hit the market have a measurable the startup capital for retail arbitrage is not limited to a particular cost.

The only requirement is that the products you intend to resell have the ability to generate a reasonable profit, in which case you can be advantageous enough to be able to win the buy box with very little startup capital. As a business person, to make a profit on your sales, there are several advantages of using Amazon to achieve this. These include:

The traffic that is active on Amazon is of high numbers, thus increasing the potential of making sales. There will be minimal or no need for marketing and advertisement, for there is a very high possibility of recurring business on Amazon. There is also the factor of needless referrals as Amazon takes care of this by making an inventory of the products they would recommend, which would increase the possibility of a customer noticing your products without necessarily been that it's the product they were searching for.

Amazon has been developed in search of a high-tech way that it provides services that are tailor-made to make running a business on the site very easy and hustle free. Apart from doing the filling of tax for the entrepreneurs, Amazon offers all the other services, including collecting tax from the sales, processing of payments from different payment options, including credit cards as well as tracking of orders. The investment that Amazon has put in the development of its functioning systems is such as that it's next to the possibility of been imitated by anyone newly venturing into private labeling, giving it the advantage of more and more re-sellers choosing it over all the other online same service providers. It also ensures that it remains highly competitive on the prices it offers not only the clients but the tradesmen as well.

The availability of FBA (Fulfillment by Amazon) saves not only money for the business persons but also on time that could have otherwise been spent on doing the packaging and making the delivery. It also curbs the stress that would come along if the entrepreneur would have to deal with shipping overseas, handling customer's queries and complains as well as taking care of returns. This also means that as the third-party seller, you will need to worry not of the available limited storage space available, so one is free to trade in as many numbers as they desire.

Amazon has been known to provide services and products that are of a wide variety with the availability of very pocket-friendly delivery charges. The experience of shopping on Amazon has been rated as a user-friendly, trustworthy state of the art service with delivery options that can be trusted.

Life, as it is, is already a strenuous undertaking. Shopping should be an enjoyable experience that is ambiguity free. The ease at which customers can shop at Amazon creates an advantage in the possibility of the customer going back to shop on the same site. Thus, in turn, increases the likelihood of making sales-generating into profits.

When beginning to sell on Amazon, as a trader one is an upfront acquainted with the fees that will be charged during trading, which are only after making a sale and are well specified while determining your price.

Private Labeling

Private labeling refers to the selling of a product by a manufacturer by using a product name provided by the retailer regularly known as Other Equipment Manufacturer (OEM). Private labeling is a tiresome, time consuming with the high risk involved. There are large sums of money required to be pumped in a while setting up the venture. This money has no guarantee not only of making a profit but making a return of the source of the capital, be it owns savings or having secured a loan.

It requires that as an entrepreneur, one is through in undertaking their research, which will include the gaps in the market as well as the cost-benefit analysis to establish the viability of the intended products. Also, identify a reliable industry or factory with the responsibility for product production. It also requires that one develops a unique identification of their product, which can be in the form of a logo. Investing in labeling as well as packaging, which will then need investment to take care of how the products will move from the manufacturing company to get to the end consumer, not forgetting the need to establish a storage place for the products. With the successful establishment of a private label, the possibility of immediately making an income is minimal compared to the possibility of doing so in retail arbitrage.

Disadvantages of Private Labeling

Low Orders

By the sole reason that the products are not known to the consumers, the number of sales made could be really low, which will translate to the retailer's unwillingness to high stock numbers of the products. This is also the case for the manufacturers responsible for the production of your product, for they would not want to be in a position of having too much dead stock in their factory. O curb this, there is a need to create awareness, which will often come at an extra cost as well as time-consuming. Marketing is a strenuous, expensive, and time-consuming activity. With low orders, the possibility of making not only profits but also returns is minimal, which is one of the major reasons as to why tradesmen prefer in trading with the already existing brands with ready markets.

Dead Stock

With the introduction of a new product, one is not sure if the consumers will prefer the products to the already existing brands. It gets to a scenario where the private label is not selling as presumed, leading to the retailer accumulating products that are not selling. It is even of higher risk if the products get to their expiry dates as this would mean losses not only to the retailer as well as to the producer. This will negatively affect the growth of the private label as, in most cases, private labels do not accept returns as compared to the branded ones where one can make a return and be compensated on the capital lost.

Perception from Consumers

Creating a culture of trust from the consumers of your product is not an easy task. Consumers mostly tend to purchase the products they had used before and discovered to work for them. With a private label, there is a tendency to believe that they are not the best quality and thus don't believe that they will get the value for their money. It is, therefore, of great necessity to conduct market research to have information of the kind of products that your targeted audience prefers, the quality of the products that they regularly use that are already available in the market to make sure that your product will also be competitive in the market.

This undertaking is an expensive one, and it still does not guarantee that your product will get the desired reception. It also does not guarantee that your product will match the already existing products as it may need time to perfect the skills of production both from the owner in the sourcing of the best raw material and also from the producer/manufacturer in learning to improve the manufacturing.

Private Labeling Trading on Amazon

This requires that one has a registered and authorized trademark for trade. This will require that the trademark be not in existence.

Disadvantages of Selling Private Labels on Amazon

Products that are sold under private labels are usually at lower prices as compared to the existing brands, which therefore means that the tradesman will have low profits even before putting into consideration the capital invested.

A high number of private labeled products are an imitation of the already existing brands, and in such, there is no uniqueness of the products.

While selling the private labels on Amazon, it means that one is responsible for the packaging as well as the designing, which has very high risks involved and too much money required to be pumped into the business.

The level of trust that consumers have on private labels is very low compared to the known, already existing brands. This negatively affects the business as it will have low sales translating to low profits.

It is time-consuming to come up with a brand as much as it will take to market it and make it known to the consumers. Results have been known to take a long time to show.

As a trader, one is entirely dependent on the manufacturer with the hope of producing products that are of good quality, at a good timing, and of the right quantities.

To be successful in trading in a private label on Amazon requires that one has vast prior knowledge in trading online. The process is ambiguous, for there are several considerations to make, ranging from deciding the goods to trade into making an inventory of the same online. It is also highly dependent on your initial capital that one is ready to invest in. It requires one to practice patience as it can take quite a long time to be able to achieve the desired results. The ability to succeed or fail on private label trading is based on how good, or poor one is in online trading.

Retail arbitrage is a business model that is known to bring together the advantageous factors of different modes of business. The period of having your money lying on a particular product as one is not limited to a limited production as they are free to trade in different products as they can source them at better prices. Every business, whether it is a side hustle or your main source of income, requires all the advantages it can receive to make it a success. One of the ways with not only minimal risks involved but also offering a busy platform is venturing into the already existing marketplaces such as Amazon. It is because of the many reasons listed above that many people prefer retail arbitrage to the private labels' method.

Chapter 8: Understanding of Retail Arbitrage on Amazon

Retail arbitrage is a very simple concept where you purchase products from retail stores such as Target, Home Depot, or Walmart and resell the same through online market platforms such as eBay or Amazon, at a profit. You get these products mostly from clearance racks in the retail stores. The most suitable items for retail arbitrage are those that are on sale since they come with a significant discount, much lower than the retail price. You might be asking yourself if it's possible to earn an extra income via retail arbitrage; well, the answer is, Yes. Some of the most common marketplaces where you can sell your items through retail arbitrage include Etsy, Facebook Marketplace, Walmart.com, Jet, eBay, OfferUp, Amazon, and many more.

How Retail Arbitrage on Amazon works

Retail arbitrage works by buying products at lower prices and reselling them on Amazon; you must account for shipping costs and marketplace fees. For instance, if you purchase a product for $9 in the retail stores and sell it for $23.99 via Amazon, you will be paid $17 if a client purchases your item. In this particular example, your $9 earns you a profit of $8; this is the simple process that can help you make substantial amounts of cash from Amazon; it's the best avenue to give you a head start in selling online if you are a beginner. Retail arbitrage is a low-risk business idea, and it's almost a guarantee that if you choose the right products, you will earn profits from the start.

Reasons Why Customers Pay More on Discounted Prices

In retail arbitrage, there are some instances when you will come across customers willing to pay more on discounted prices. There are various reasons why certain customers can pay more for products, even when similar products are available at lower prices. Some of these reasons include:

Your Items Are Easier to Purchase

Customers don't like the idea of having to through complicated payment and purchasing options. Many customers are always ready to pay an extra fee if your purchase process proves to be easier and hustle free.

You Deliver Your Products Quickly and on Time

Human beings will always appreciate instant gratification, especially if they're paying for the products. Gratifying your client's needs sooner than your competitors will always pay off. Timely delivery is a key factor in customer retention and satisfaction. Some customers would rather pay more and get their products on the spot than pay less and wait for a month to get the same product.

Your Products Help in Polishing the Customer's Reputation

Some customers purchase fancy-branded goods to make them feel and appear wealthy, for luxury; some people will pay more to get a product from a certain brand. The same product from a different could be available at a lower price, but certain people want products from popular brands.

Your Products Have Lower Costs of Ownership

At times, it's not the price that only matters, but the money and time that you will spend after purchasing your product. For instance, an iPad is costly than the usual Windows netbook, but it needs less maintenance; this makes it much cheaper at the end of it all. Customers will prefer to purchase the iPad instead of the Windows netbook though the purchasing price is higher.

You Have Friendly Customer Service

Customers prefer to take the risk and purchase products at higher prices with the guarantee that they will get super customer service if the need arises. It is disheartening to purchase products at lower prices, but in case of a problem, you can't get any assistance, or you get substandard assistance altogether.

Having a Likeable Personality to the Customers

Human beings prefer conducting business with people who have friendly personalities. Building a rapport with your customers is vital in customer relationships. You will have the guarantee of repeat customers, keeping your competitors at bay. People will always prefer buying products at higher prices in friendly environments, even when similar products are available at lower prices, in unfriendly environments.

Customers Need Something Besides Your Products from You

If a customer is hoping to make extra gains from you, say hoping that you can give him/her a job in your business, or even a relationship, he will be willing to pay more for your products, even in instances where similar products are readily available at lower prices.

The Customer Is Experiencing Rapid Expansion

Customers who are experiencing rapid growth in terms of business want to use all available opportunities to their advantage; they will rarely have time to window-shop for cheaper products as long as you can deliver and help them in satisfying their demand.

Tips on How You Can Implement Discounts Profitably

Defining Your Objectives

Implementing discount pricing without goals is a mistake that you can make in retail arbitrage that will make you run into huge losses; have a clear purpose before deciding on your discount percentage. Ask yourself if you're offering discounts to attract new clients or to get repeat customers, or if you intend to lure customers who haven't bought any product from you for a while. When crafting your discount, these are some of the questions that you should address. Different objectives require different forms of discounts. For instance, if you aim to acquire new customers, you'll have to employ more forceful tactics, i.e., store-wide sales or loss leaders, to lure many people. However, if you're aiming at re-engaging customers who haven't bought any product for a while, you can personalize your discounts and offer custom-made deals.

Having a clear definition of what you hope to achieve by offering discounts will help you in deciding on what to offer on a discount, when, and the discount percentage you need to offer.

Segmenting Shoppers and Tailoring Offers Accordingly

When offering discount pricing, you need to consider your customers' purchase histories and preferences, which will help you to increase conversions. Segmenting your customer base is vital to help you in marketing and selling to them profitably.

One way that you can achieve this is by establishing customer profiles. Building profiles showcasing shopping habits and price sensitivity of various customers and employing them as tools to decide on the discounting pricing to offer different customers is important.

Ensuring That Your Timing Is Right

When you plan to give offers and discounts, timing is as crucial as relevance. Giving pricing discounts at the right time, i.e., when there is a demand from the customers, will play a big role in increasing your profit margins and conversion rates. You need to pay attention when customers are purchasing your products, for example, you need to know when you make more sales and which products are in more demand at what time. It's the only way that you will decide on the perfect time to offer discount pricing.

Always note questions that customers ask when purchasing or asking about your products; this will give you direction on what you can buy next or what you can add to your existing stock. If a customer asks for newborn clothes, you can estimate that in six months she will need more clothes; you could ask for her contacts and call her in six months to tell her that you have clothes for a six months old.

How Can You Use Discount Pricing Strategies to Increase Sales?

When small startups are looking into ways with which they can increase their sales, the most common approach that they use is by offering discounts. The downside to offering discounts to attract more customers is that you may end up incurring losses or damaging your brand reputation. However, you can do proper discount pricing to increase your sales; it can ensure that your products will sell at the lower prices in larger volumes.

You will have to create solid objectives and target various approaches to achieve them. There are various advantages of discount pricing, and they can act as guidelines when setting your prices; some clients will opt to pay more for similar products.

A major advantage of discount pricing policies is that setting price discounts can help in increasing sales volumes to your online venture by enticing more clients. It makes your customers feel good; they relax and become happier, and it brings long term benefits. Customers are likely to come back in the future even when you won't be offering any discounts. You may make a few losses at the beginning when you offer discounts, but the same clients will come back and purchase your products at higher prices, as long as you offer quality products.

When you offer a discount, the chances are high that customers won't go through the hustle of comparing your products with similar products that are selling at higher prices. New customers will end up buying your products, which will give you a footing in retail arbitrage.

How Can You Make Customers to Pay Full Prices on Discounted Prices?

The main advantage of using discount pricing is that it plays a key role in accelerating sales volumes to your online products since it is very enticing to customers. You can only make maximum profits from discount prices by ensuring that your customers will pay more for discounted prices. You can achieve this by setting your goals before settling on your discount prices. Before deciding on the discount strategy that you will use, it's good that you develop your primary goal first.

You will make better decisions in determining how much discount you can give for certain products, how you intend to do the marketing, and which is your target market. Always price your products in almost similar price ranges as your competitors, as long as you get some profit. Also, try and offer the same quality at lower prices than your competitors; by doing so, customers will start having trust in your brand, and the next time you won't be having discounts, they will still source their products from you.

Goals You Should Aim at Achieving When You Offer Discount Pricing to Your Customers

Acquiring New Clients

You should offer discounts to attract new customers; customers tend to buy more products at discount prices since they associate lower risks with discounts. Also, if you are offering discounts for a certain duration, new clients will have the urge to try your products and services before the discount period expires.

Increasing Your Sales

Another important goal when setting discount pricing is to sell your products in larger volumes. You may attract a few customers who will purchase your products in large volumes; this means going after volume sales, and encouraging clients to purchase as many products as they can before they leave the marketplace page.

Gaining Repeat Clients

Getting repeat customers is different from acquiring new clients since it needs a different business mindset. You can use discount pricing to gain loyal customers instead of enticing new buyers who will only purchase your products and never buy from you again. Research has shown that more than 55% of potential customers get into loyalty programs with the sole aim of enjoying discounts on purchase.

Doing Away with Old Inventory

At times, you may have to offer discounts to clear your old stock, which will create room for other products. You may have the urge to update your product line or focus on quicker moving products, yet you have old stagnant stock. Selling these products at a discount will ensure that they move quickly to facilitate the introduction of fresh products that are likely to give you more profit.

Discount pricing is among the most effective and popular ways of driving sales in online marketplaces. Research shows that offering discounts is the number one profit strategy for retailers on online marketplaces such as Amazon. However, the same strategy can work against your venture if you execute discounts wrongly; you could end up attracting the wrong audience or slaying your profits, i.e., those that will purchase your products only when you are offering discounts.

Various Strategies and Business Models Used in Amazon

A business model refers to the approach of transaction that a tradesperson can employ to be able to develop, deliver as well as seize opportunities for generating profit.

A business strategy, on the other hand, refers to the soft input in the business. Again, these are the ideas and decisions to help in the attainment of the goals and objectives of the company. They are the techniques that are uniquely designed to enable the business to increase the traffic of sales and remain ahead of the competition.

The internet has come to change the way people make transactions, and it is a prime platform for anyone in business with the desire to grow their business. The easiness at which one can make a startup for an online business is another factor that is encouraging more and more entrepreneurs to invest online. Technology at the disposal of their website is an enticing factor for every business person. It is a company in the combination of technology and the retailing business.

Its source of income is primarily through commissions and charges incurred by tradesmen. This is through the facilitation of getting clients as it provides a sure market platform with worthwhile experience to both the customer and the trader. Its associate programs are also a more significant source of income as they have bigger commissions incurred by traders with the availability of better services and more sales. Amazon has also developed and traded Kindle, which is a device that enables the reading of e-books. With the availability of this device, there is also the creating of books for sale. Fortunately, this generates a huge percentage of income as there are very minimal costs incurred with exclude publishing costs. Finally, Amazon has created a subscription model where, as a user, one can access movies from streamlines through the internet. This also offers the clients the possibility of their purchased products been delivered faster than the usual delivery chains. The income of Amazon is, therefore, expounded with the option of the site investing in other areas, which is very much possible considering the high technology they employ.

However, in an online transaction, there are several models of business that one can employ. These includes:

- **AdSense** - The simplest available model that only requires creating content and moving numbers.
- **Amazon affiliate** - Using Amazon associate programs by building portfolios and transacting
- **Affiliate marketing** - Discovering the associate that there can be of the products you intend to sell and developing a network to generate sales.
- **Ecommerce** - Having an online store where all the business transactions are operated online

Amazon Business Strategy

Amazon is deniably one of the gurus when it comes to making business transactions. It offers quite a huge number of potential customers, not forgetting the high-tech developed systems of its operations and the advantages it offers to entrepreneurs. While transacting on Amazon, there are different models of business that one can make use of. These include:

Amazon FBA

This is a package that enables business people to enjoy all the benefits that Amazon has to offer. From having their goods store at Amazon's warehouses to Amazon crediting their payments in their accounts from collecting the tax sales. This is a very lucrative arrangement to take advantage of.

Amazon Affiliate

Amazon has been in operation for a long time now. Therefore this has enabled it to gain the trust not only of the shoppers but of the business people as well, which in turn translates to having high visitations and transactions. Business people tend to make more and more use, as this is a promising site for the growth of their business. Another advantage is that it is quite easy to set up to the point that even a beginner in online business is easily able to make a start out.

Reselling

This is the highly utilized business model on Amazon. It involves entrepreneurs purchasing products in large quantities. That is, acquiring wholesale to be in a position to obtain the goods at low prices then selling the products at a higher price. Therefore, this method requires that the entrepreneur arranges the storage services of the products as well as shipping them to the clients when ordered. It is also the responsibility of the entrepreneur to do the packaging as well as developing an inventory of the products in storage.

Dropshipping

Unlike in the reselling business model, this does not necessitate the need to purchase the products in large quantities and storing them, but instead, one makes a listing of the products in Amazon and notifies the suppliers when there is a pending order for them to do the delivery. The trick in this model is finding a supplier that will agree to have the products branded with your business or company name as well as having good bargains to make an income considering that the purchases have not been made on a wholesale basis. As an entrepreneur, you are also responsible for handling all the customer queries, notifying the supplier of when an order is placed, and giving specifications of the locations to be delivered to. This can be a tiresome and time-consuming activity.

Manufacturing

As the original producer of a product, and you can get avail of the products in the warehouse, trading on Amazon is very lucrative. This is because one is able to eliminate all the third parties and, therefore, able to have all the profit to themselves. However, the disadvantage of this product is the headaches brought about by the arrangement to make deliveries and having to deal with customers directly. Setting up your product on Amazon is another factor to consider, as it means you will be the first to make the inventory of the products on Amazon. This necessitates that you do a thorough description of the items with clear photographic representations and that including Amazon SEO. It is necessary to take into consideration the employment of Amazon FBA to reduce the amount of time spent on worrying about delivery to the customers and customer care services to be offered.

Private Label

This is a model that an entrepreneur privatizes a common already existing label like soft drinks by coming up with a new design or a unique packaging and hiring a manufacturer to do the production. The trick here is realizing the less competitive products and has high demands in the market then make a unique maybe labeling. It is also essential to keep in mind that, in so doing, one should not legally violate the already existing brands. Make an inventory of the products on Amazon under the private label with the possibility of selling it at a lower price compared to the existing brands.

Retail Arbitrage

This is the most popular employed model of business on Amazon. It involves sourcing for extremely low prices in instances that, for example, a company is almost closing down and is disposing of their products and then selling the products at higher prices. It only requires that one makes arrangements of the products to be delivered to the Amazon's warehouses and resting as Amazon takes care of the inventory, packaging, shipping, and tax collection form sales as well as crediting the money to the accounts of the businessmen.

Liquidation

This is close to retail arbitrage, but the only difference is that in this model, as an entrepreneur, you only get the products after the company has closed down. However, unlike retail arbitrage where the products are sourced at the time, the company is almost closing down. The trick to employ here is realizing that most of the products that will be available are mostly probably rejects. Thus, and the possibility of them not been able to be sold high. Therefore, one has to be extra careful when choosing the items. Be ready to adjust your selling prices by offering discounts. For example, of having to giveaways as you can be sure to face stiff competition from the other "better" products in terms of the condition they are in.

Amazon strategy

Amazon Customers

The mission and vision of this company are aimed at the satisfaction of the customer to be able to have repeat business. Therefore, for this very reason, the company has invested in the delivery process as well as the technology to realize its achievement.

This has been done by availing very competitive prices for the customer, making it remain ahead of the competition while also having a wide range of products at the disposal of the customer with the convenience of shipment. By being able to have loyalty from its customers, it has been key to the continued running of the business.

Amazon has also enabled the ability for the customers to analyze the quality of the products they are offering. It also gives the information about the manufacturer of the item just in case there are any say religious restrictions that can be necessary to be known to the consumer say, for example, a Muslim purchasing an item from a manufacturer who does pork too.

Exclusion of shipping charges on a particular range of amount spend is used to encourage the customers to shop more to enjoy this service while at the same time making sure that the desired profit is achieved even if the shipment is free.

Amazon has remained convenient by making available any new listings of products, by giving an estimate dates of the shipment to reach to the consumer, giving the available shipment options as well as enabling tracking of delivery of products shipping.

When it comes to the use of Kindle say for streaming or downloads, Amazon has made sure that the speed of such accessibility is very high for the customer's convenience.

The Focus on Technology

The technology employed at Amazon is also another primary strategy in doing business. The software enables the smooth running of the business from the beginning to the end with such simplicity of being it shopping or selling. This has, in turn, enabled Amazon to stay ahead of the competition and have more and more traffic in sales.

Competition Factor

Be it convenience, reliability pricing of products, available stocks privately customized goods, shipment options and charges, customer relations services, speed in the delivery of services, and the overall customer feedback in relation, and Amazon has strived to be second to none. The quality of either the products or services to be availed in Amazon is also thoroughly scrutinized to remain competitive.
The knowledge that your competitors can bring your business to a close and they strive to make sure that this does not happen has enabled Amazon to be the site to go to, whether in selling or buying.

Media Sales

Amazon, unlike the rest, makes Google advertisements and creates banners for different brands. Also, this generates huge sales even though it has been said to congest the sites.

Marketing

Although little is known on the information on how Amazon carries out its marketing, the techniques it employs include mass media marketing as well as outdoor marketing. There is also the use of sponsored search and purpose of affiliate programs and online marketing as well as email campaigns. Although the exclusion of shipping charges on a specific set amount spent while shopping is not used as a marketing strategy, it seems to me be a very lucrative marketing model.
 In summary;
Despite Amazon having made a startup as just a books store in the 1990s, it has grown to become a market for anything that exists under the sun. Customers have great experiences shopping at Amazon, while business people have been able to increase their income by use of the same website. It is arguably true to say that the success of the site is based on the business model and strategies they use, which is so convincing to both the buyer and the seller.

Chapter 9: Tips and Tricks to Earn Passive Income with Retail Arbitrage

Passive income refers to an income you regularly receive, even without working or putting more effort into it. In other words, you can say, passive income is the flow of income you are regularly earning but with little effort. More so, sometimes, we may call it progressive passive income, especially when the earner is still rendering some little effort to make it grow. Examples of such kind of revenues include rental incomes, book royalties, bonds, stock dividends, and much more.

Types of Passive Activities:

- Property income cash flow: This involves all types of profits coming from rental and capital ownership. Also, it includes income from real estate and to some point, those interest you earn from your financial assets.
- Any form of trade or business where one doesn't require to maintain his effort every day. In this

situation, you can go even for a year without doing anything, but in the end, you will end up earning some income.
- Another type involves royalties. Royalties form part of payments that a company gives you to use your property. This can be books, videos, or even music.

The funniest thing with passive income is that it can generate itself while you are doing nothing at all. You can be sleeping while the passive income is filling your account. A good scenario is where you are working, and at the same time, you have a listed eBook in your Amazon account. The buyers will purchase this without necessarily your presence. That is the company such as Amazon will handle everything for you. Passiveincome has several benefits that you need to know before venturing into how you can create it in Amazon retail arbitrage.

Significance of Passive Income

- Establishes an opportunity for early retirement
- Accelerates wealth-building goals
- It acts as a backup especially when your formal contract expires or when you lose your job

- Always provides an alternative income in a situation where you can't work anymore.

However, creating this type of income is not just easy. That is, it will take you both time and a large volume of capital, which will bring little return from the beginning. The creation of this income involves a series of frustrations and a massive learning curve. Fortunately, it is the most profitable venture you can always engage in since this income will spread in all of your scheduled times. Some of these passive incomes have been seen even to offer financial support to several generations ahead. Due to this reason, you will realize many people prefer using retail arbitrage to generate this type of income within the Amazon.

Again, you need to understand that passive income is a slow process of generating income, but you should not fully rely on it since some are eventually unpredictable. A good example is where you have listed a book for selling in Amazon without proper marketing. Your book might take several months before you start earning from it. Sometimes, this might again take quite a number of times. In the case where you had utterly relied on it, you might face some serious financial challenges. In this situation, you will have to look at the marketing tips that will enable you to walk through the stiff completion from the other competitors.

Therefore, let's take a look at some of the tips and tricks someone can use to make excess passive income with retail arbitrage.

Tips on How to Earn Passive Income with Retail Arbitrage

There are several tips that you can eventually use to create passive income in retail arbitrage. Remember, on most occasions, and retail arbitrage depends on the difference in prices of commodities. The different prices will initiate an inflow of income. Assume you have seen a product in Kindle or other sites retailing at $4 while in Amazon, it goes for $35, you can take that opportunity. That is a good profit you can make within a short period, especially when you can manage to have excess stock. Below are retail arbitrage tips we can use to create more passive income in the Amazon:

Prefer Scanning for Several Items While Sourcing

Scanning for products will enable you to understand whether you are dealing with a product based on its inventory levels or not. However, some products have wholesale, while others have private labels. Therefore, at the clearance site, you need to go for those items that will give you wholesale options.

You will then use this to fill your stock within your retail arbitrage account in the Amazon. In this situation, you will be in a position to have excess inventories, which translates to excess sales in the coming future. Fortunately, this will create more wealth in terms of passive income.

Try Asking Several Questions About the Products You Are Sourcing

Ask, and you shall receive a close-set term used in the previous generations who managed to live before us. It well stated that a closed mouth will never be fed or will not get fed in any way. Asking about something doesn't make you stupid, or neither will it lowers your reputation. Ironically, if you fail to ask the burning questions about the trending products on clearance lists, how will you get to know the answer? There are several ways to undertake this strategy in retail arbitrage, and one of them is to request a discount, especially when the products have been delivered to you. Remember, these products have been discounted at the purchasing point, and by asking for more discounts on the already discounted items, will make you earn much. This, in the end, will create an excess flow of passive income. Asking helps a lot not only to the buyer but also to the sellers who want to clear off their products. Always, clearance of products fetches a low marked price. Ask for help still even though, at some point, you might fail to get the expected reply, but asking will help you a lot. Remember, in any business, and many are willing to help since they are also aware you might be helpful in the long run.

No More Comfort Zone

The comfort zone means the same spot in life that gives you the same feeling every time. That is the exact place where you always reside or where you go. We all have comfort zones, especially in business. This is where we shall go and restock our inventories. Meaning, having the same inventories with the same marked price and reselling the inventories with the same selling price you had set initially. In the end, you will realize the same amount of passive income over a specific period.

However, changing your comfort zone will allow you to change the way you think about new products. You will be making changes in life, and new things always come with new opportunities. It is through this that you might scan a good product within the clearing shelves. Here their prices will be low as compared to the prices being offered on Amazon. You can strike that deal and never hesitate to have enough time picking excess, especially if the prices are manageable. Therefore, with enough capital, you will be in a position to make more purchases, which will help you restock your products. In the long run, this will yield an enormous kind of passive income.

Never Overlook the Oversize Items

Many people will always try to avoid products with oversize shapes, especially those that weigh much in terms of weight. You can strike a deal by venturing into these since it will lack stiff completion. In most cases, as long as you can make a substantial benefit from the sale, then you need not avoid it. It will lead to excess profits in the future even though it will require some extra effort to manage this. Oversize items include big-box items that demand a more extensive space during shipping. They might consist of playset items, vehicles, and even spare parts of some merchandise. However, as long as there is a profit that you will make, try your best by getting into it. This will eventually realize much more profit when you are not putting more effort into the near future.

You Should Be Nice

Every business person should struggle as much as possible to be kind even without being reminded. In most clearing sites, store managers always have the power of dealing with the products within their stores. If you are that person who will always struggle to leave some unsolved tasks within the store, they might fail to consider you next time. Consideration implies many things when it comes to retail business. When you are nice to these store managers, you might get the following:

- Getting your orders before the Black Friday
- Having additional discounts without asking
- Price matching clearance items

Concentrate on the Overlooked Items

There are items that people usually overlook since they fail to have the barcodes and other required information.
A good example might be booked. Published books are always displayed for sale, and if the book publishing companies have the expected traffic, the demands will rise. However, retailers might fail to source for this since those who managed, failed to have it due to lack of enough information. These lazy scanners will take it back to the shelves and fail to source it. Therefore, a book like this when you source it correctly, you might end up making an excess profit. Again, when you do it in large quantities, it will create a sizeable passive income in the long run. More so, you should avoid issues of overlooking products just because it doesn't have enough information That is required.

Change Your Sourcing Time

Prefer sourcing late at night. This is because, at night, you will be able to identify the products that people love. Those empty shelves will guide you to fill your inventories since the probability of selling will be high. At night, the shelves are almost being filled for the next day selling and looking at it before being filled, will instill in you enough information about what you are supposed to have in the next day.

Don't Overlook Common Items

There are some items that you need not overlook since most companies sell them, and they are always trending in terms of sales. These products are always unique, and mostly, you will realize many people prefer them, whether they are in large quantities or not.

Prefer Specific Focus

Getting into stores, you might get overwhelmed due to the large volume of products that are kept there. Trying to focus on every item might be overwhelming, and this can prevent you from achieving your main focus. Therefore, the best way to undertake this is to concentrate on specific tasks only. By doing this, you will be in a win/win situation where next time you will still manage to concentrate on the other ones you fail to focus on at this time.

Be Keen on Your Specialties

A store consists of various products that start from households to groceries. On most occasions, you will find both new items and the ones you are used to. You can keep your specific items and at the same time, buy one new item for testing. In case it might be not good or not the way you had expected, you will feel much ok for buying only one instead of ten.

Therefore, in a quick view, tips, and tricks in earning passive income will always depend on people. As a retailer, especially within the Amazon FBA, all tricks and tips might work for you. However, you have to put extra effort into achieving this. Passive income doesn't just come as easy as some might think but involves a chain of process. This chain will always be thorny from the beginning since you will invest much before starting to get passive income. A case study is where someone has invested in a real estate where the initial capital is worth billions. He cannot realize this passive income until people start occupying his premises.

That is the rental income which forms part and parcel of the passive income will only begin to flowing in after some quiet periods. Fortunately, the best thing is that he will be earning now without much effort. Real estate investing is the best form of passive income that is done by most wealthy people who have enough wealth and capital to furnish. On the other hand, there are some real passive incomes we can get through retail arbitrage.

Conclusion

It is important to understand that anyone can sell on Amazon. It doesn't matter whether it is something that you purchased in wholesale and a product you no longer need or something you have made. It means that if you list your product on Amazon, you enjoy other services like advanced shipment, earning more sales from the vast number of Amazon customers. Amazon's FBA program enables you to grow your business and reach more people. You may not have achieved this had you decided to use other platforms. Be sensitive to the ever-changing customer need and provide products that can compete in the market. Amazon does not limit companies, even the small ones.

Each business is allowed to enjoy the most extensive and most fulfilling customer base across the globe. Customers are also most likely to trust your products and services if you are associated with Amazon. FBA enhances integration with Big-commerce, thus a significant market share. It helps you build customer feedback quickly, which is very useful and get your reputation that your product can be trusted. You let Amazon handle customer complaints. There are so many people selling on Amazon every day. At the same time complaints are also very many, and sometimes it is good to help someone do that on your behalf.

Globalization has made the world a global village. Shipping individual products overseas can be an excruciating and expensive task. For this reason, Amazon makes the shipment for different orders from different companies at the same time. Amazon is also a trusted brand, and this advantage can limit the customers' doubt even when you have just launched a new product. Entrepreneurs who have discovered the benefits of Amazon FBA are using it to their advantage. If you do not understand how it works, even after reading this book, continue doing more research on the subject. The information received will help you grow your business and offer better products to your customers. Anything good also comes with disadvantages, with Amazon FBA; however, the benefits far outweigh the demerits.

There are simple things that can improve how you introduce your product to the market. That is something as simple as packaging and description. Introduce sales and promotions strategies that work. It can create a high impact on sales and introduce new customers. Do not hesitate to add a new product on the market. Once you do your market research, refer to this book again for some tips. Always understand that knowledge is power, so never stop researching on a product. Sometimes also you may introduce a product. After doing everything right you may still realize that the product does not pick as you expected. When this happens, go back, and find out what you did not do right. Incorporate promotion strategies.

Amazon FBA can and has created financial freedom for many entrepreneurs. Companies have made billions of dollars trading with Amazon every year. The majority of the companies use Amazon FBA. Online business is expected to continue growing steadily due to a change in people's lifestyle. For this reason, it is good to learn about Amazon FBA.

www.ingramcontent.com/pod-product-compliance
Lightning Source LLC
Chambersburg PA
CBHW071409210526
45465CB00001B/302